The

The Queen Boss Rise

15 EMPOWERING LESSONS TO CATAPULT YOUR IMPACT, MONEY, AND FREEDOM

A Compilation by

ERICA STEPTEAU

i

The Queen Boss Rise

ISBN: 9781084196285

DEDICATION

This book is dedicated to every ambitious entrepreneur in the world putting their heart on the line each and every day. The we do as Service Providers requires a sound mind and lots of tenacity. I pray this book gives you inspiration, peace of mind, practical tips, and EVIDENCE that you too can achieve consistent wealth in your business. Cheers to more Impact, Money, and Freedom!

The Queen Boss Rise

CONTENTS

The Queen Boss Rise

ACKNOWLEDGMENTS

I would like to acknowledge each of the fifteen beautiful co-authors who has allowed this project to exist. Because of their dedication, transparency, and tenacity, we have produced a masterpiece and legacy for our generations to come. I have witnessed my Queens overcoming very tragic circumstances such as job loss, family death, depression, anxiety, miscarriages, divorces, and other unforeseen life events. These Queens have kept pressing forward and some decided to pause, reflect, and rediscover themselves. Regardless, the journey continues, and each co-author has taught me something new about myself and my business processes. Powerful content has been developed from our interactions and their stories were shared in this project to provide evidence to you as the reader.

Further acknowledgement goes to our Book Publisher: Dr. Jackie Evans Phillips, Book Cover Designer: Allison Arnett, Editor: Dr. Karen Maxfield-Lunkin, Life Coach: Lindsey Vertner. Each one of these dynamic ladies played a huge role in working directly with each author to ensure their story was from a healing space, organized, and concise. This project would have not been possible without these dedicated experts.

The Queen Boss Rise

The Queens are Rising

Erica Stepteau

Website: TenaciousQueenAcademy.com

Facebook: Erica Stepteau

Instagram: Erica_Stepteau

LinkedIn: Erica Stepteau

Chapter 1

The Queens are Rising
Erica Stepteau

Is this you? You are ready for a major up level in your life and ready to put action in, but just don't know where to start. You struggle with consistency in many departments in your life and business. You find yourself jumping from one thought to another feeling confused, empty, and purposeless. Yet, you hear a small whisper saying, "There is more."

NEARLY 40% OF ALL U.S. BUSINESSES ARE WOMEN-OWNED AND BY 2025 IT IS PROJECTED TO RISE TO 55% BASED ON THE CENSUS BUREAU

These statistics prove that more women are building up the courage to step into their brilliance and become powerful **Influencers** in their industries. The **Queen Boss Rise** is a movement inspiring woman all around the world to use their unique gifts to become the CEO of their life, despite the distractions along the way.

I am here to declare: You are a **Queen Boss**. You might not know it yet; you might feel alone or small or not enough. But I am here to tell you that it is time to shake out your hair and grab your crown. Your power is based in the tenacity of your heart, because only with unflinching faith and relentless action, can you claim your throne.

A true queen has grace, poise, confidence, intelligence and a warrior spirit because no matter what, she will stand for her kingdom, her legacy, her truth, and no one will deny it of her.

It's time to be the tenacious woman God called you to be and build Generational Wealth.

Most of the time, it's our emotional baggage and gremlins preventing us from stepping into our power. You are a **Queen Boss** and this book's purpose is to empower women to push beyond thoughts of scarcity, past failures, potential obstacles, or lack of resources. In this book, you will find stories from 15 women who were brave enough to lead a tribe, bold enough to be on the front line, and brazen enough to speak her truth when the world was encouraging her to remain "status quo."

There was a time in my life when it was hard to get out of bed in the morning. I was lost and overwhelmed, I felt defeated, and felt beaten down by depression. It was right after my third miscarriage and I found myself throwing fits, tossing things, and drinking during the day just to mask my emotions which left me feeling completely helpless and alone. Every day was a battle; I was lost in a fog and no longer living. I was in survival mode and not even able to recognize who I was in the mirror.

But then, something changed. I was reminded that I had greatness within me. I had forgotten that truth somewhere along the way, but in a moment, I remembered. In that moment, I decided I needed to change my life so that I could claim the phenomenal life that was destined for me.

As I was emerging from my brokenness and owning my power, I was scrolling online and came across Baylor Barbee's chess approach to life and business. What he said woke me up and paved the way to the rest of my journey.

> "Every day you define your role: how you move, how you operate, how you plan. In chess, a pawn can move one space, at most two spaces. A Queen, on the other hand, can move in ANY Direction, as far as she wants. Think about your life. There are no limitations on how much you can accomplish in a day. No one will ever tell you you've gone too far today, you've accomplished too much, and you must stop here. We place those limitations on ourselves sometimes. We don't strive for royalty; we settle for being pawns.
>
> God doesn't want that for us. God wants us to move about freely. He wants us to cover 'the entire board.' That's why He put us on it. In Chess, inexperienced players usually sacrifice their pawns early in the game and try and protect 'the

important pieces.' Losing a pawn doesn't affect us, but losing a Bishop, a Queen, and especially a King, hurts us. In life, we define our roles based on the decisions we make. Too many people lead careless, uncalculated lives, running right into devastation.

Look at people you admire and look up to. There's a good chance they live their lives Brave, Bold, and Brazen. They invested in a solid support group around them. They work well with others. They make calculated moves and they plan very well. Aside from that, when it's time to make a move in life, they strike hard and cover a lot of ground. You can do the same. You CAN be the Queen on this Chess Board of Life. All it takes is a change in your mindset. You must live your life as a piece that matters, and subsequently, people around you will start treating you as such."

Inspired by this principle of living as a Queen, I radically overhauled my life and have helped many women to do the same within my Coaching programs. I am here to remind you, whoever you are and wherever you are, you have infinite power within you, even if you don't feel it right now. That power is what you need to tap into in order to claim your inheritance and be a Queen Boss.

It's your time to catapult your Impact, Money, and Freedom!

Erica Stepteau

CEO/Master Sales Coach

Tenacious Queen Academy, LLC

The Queen Boss Rise

A Wrecked Self-Worth

Lindsey Vertner

Website: www.LindseyVertner.com

Email: GetHappy@LindseyVertner.com.

Live event updates: www.TheUnleashedWoman.net

Chapter 2

A Wrecked Self-Worth

Lindsey Vertner

"It is your responsibility to find the purpose in your pain. Otherwise, you're suffering for nothing!"

- Lindsey Vertner

Have you ever watched a scary movie where the main character is going about their everyday life, and then suddenly, they wake up in total darkness and can't move? Well, in 2007, that was me!

Fortunately, I wasn't in a scary movie (although most people would beg to differ, given the circumstance). Let me rewind.

On May 13, 2007, I headed back home after visiting my hometown of Evansville, Indiana. I had surprised my mother with a weekend of Mother's Day festivities. It was a beautiful, sunny day, and I was living life to the fullest. I remember saying my goodbyes, grabbing lunch, and hopping on the highway for my three-hour drive home. And then...

Darkness.

I tried to get up. I couldn't move.

Why can't I move?

Wait! Where am I? This is not my house.

I can't see. I don't hear anything.

As I tried to figure out what was going on, it felt as if my heart was beating out of my chest.

Have I been kidnapped? Oh, my God!

I cried out for help but didn't hear my voice. Instead, I heard myself choking. As I started to panic, I noticed the glare of the moon shining through a window that wasn't mine. Eventually, I tired myself out and fell back asleep. I woke up to the heat of the sun shining on my face.

"Oh, my goodness. That nightmare felt so real!" I thought to myself as tried to sit up.

Oh, no! I still can't move, I still can't see, and that window…

…still wasn't mine, but this time, I heard something…voices.

A woman walked up to me and asked if I knew my name, where I was, and what the date was. I wanted to answer, but my mind drew a blank. The woman proceeded to tell me that I had been in a horrible car wreck. The car I was driving looked like it was doing back flips before landing on its roof off the side of the highway. I was pronounced brain dead on the scene. I was kept alive on life support while I was sent by helicopter to Indianapolis, Indiana. Upon arrival, I was rushed into emergency surgery to relieve the pressure on my brain. I wasn't expected to make it through the night nor the next day. I would endure multiple surgeries, brain trauma, massive head injuries, crushed vertebrae, pneumonia, blood clots, hematomas, cuts, stitches, staples, a breathing tube, things I'm sure I forgot due to memory loss, and…

Paralysis.

Well, that sure explained a lot. I couldn't move because my entire left side was paralyzed. My right side was strapped down, because days before, I unconsciously kept trying to remove the tube down my throat that was keeping me breathing. Ahhhh! That explained my unheard screams. And as far as my sight, well, I've worn glasses since the first grade, and my contacts were removed during surgery.

Apparently, there's a "super" version of intensive care for the extremely severe patients. It's so intense that no one is allowed to stay the night, not even my mother. That's why no one was around to notice when I woke up in the middle of the night. Although I was left to the vices of my vivid imagination, I was extremely relieved that I, in fact, had NOT been kidnapped. My month-long hospital stint and the road to recovery weren't that bad. It was annoying, but not agonizing because I was determined to return to my normal life as a fully functioning adult. My positive outlook helped me recover quicker than what was typically expected given my injuries and condition (but that's another story for another day).

When I was removed from the breathing tube, I could barely talk. My vocal cords were damaged. To this day, I still can't scream. Initially, my mother helped me to communicate with blinking: blink once for yes, twice for no. Soon, I graduated to writing notes. Despite my notes resembling the scribbles of a toddler, I was improving. Eventually, I progressed enough to be transferred to a therapeutic hospital where I began a variety of therapies. From 7am to 6pm, seven days per week – I was doing therapy. Physical therapy, occupational therapy, shock therapy, cognitive therapy, you name it! Given my extensive list of injuries and having been pronounced brain dead multiple times, my doctors and therapists were shocked at how quickly I recovered. I do have residual back pains and a hardly noticeable limp, but my physical recovery was nothing short of miraculous. However, my emotional recovery, for lack of better terms…was a bitch!

I had always been an "A" student. I liked learning new things, and I caught on quickly. Due to the brain injuries that I sustained; the doctors informed my family that I may not be the same person when I "come to." Although my personality didn't change, my self-worth did. My focus wasn't the same. Before the accident, I loved reading…until it took me an hour to read one page. I would read the same paragraph over and over. It was like my brain didn't comprehend the words enough to move on to the next part. When talking, I would start a sentence only to completely forget what I was going to say in the middle of my words. (For this reason, I became great at "reality improv!") In conversation, people would talk to me like we had been friends forever. All the while, I was trying to figure who they were in my head. I was self-conscious about the shaved head I didn't ask for and worried if my hair would grow back over the scar tissue. My scalp resembled a traveler's map:

> "Okay, tourists! We're gonna take a right by this bumpy skull and follow this scar all the way down where you'll find the left ear. She's having a little trouble hearing out of that since the wreck, so, make sure you speak up!"

Things that previously came easy to me, I now struggled to complete. Although, I smiled and was bubbly on the outside, I was battling to understand my purpose and worth on the inside. So, when people called me "miracle woman" or "walking miracle" (and terms like that became my nickname), I felt like a fraud. As if the pressures of being a black woman weren't high enough already, I had to be a miiiiracle woman! Don't get me wrong! I was honored, but people expected great moments to happen just by being in my presence.

Whaaaat? I can't do that! That pressure combined with my own sense of pride, often caused me to not ask for help when I likely should have. I felt unworthy of the admiration I received. I even had survivor's guilt when a few people I knew passed away after my recovery (even though their passing had nothing to do with me). My family prayed, and I'm here. Their families prayed, and they're gone.

Why me? Why am I still here?

Granted, I'm grateful that God kept me, but what makes me so special? Of course, the wreck strengthened my faith, but I didn't feel any more spiritual than I did before the wreck. That only made me feel even worse because people told me that their faith was renewed due to my story. I didn't feel good enough to be THAT person.

As time went on, I started a self-improvement journey. I came to recognize that feelings of unworthiness and not being good enough were subconscious limiting beliefs. They were driving my behaviors, and I didn't even know it (hence the term "subconscious"). Everything had to be perfect. All my ducks had to be in a row. Although I was providing solutions in the real world, I was critiquing every detail and problem in my mind. I was extremely hard on myself about everything. Struggles in my marriage – what am I doing wrong? My kids acting a fool – where did I falter? My business wasn't growing fast enough – why wasn't I hustling harder?

The more I became aware of my limiting beliefs, the easier it was to identify where and how they influenced many events from my past. I was able to link it all the way back to my childhood. The absence of my father as a little girl was the beginning of my, "I'm not good enough" belief. An abusive relationship as a teenager further ingrained the belief that "I'm not good enough." Any time that I have truly struggled and every time that I was trying to up-level my success, signs of unworthiness and not being good enough were present. It wasn't until my car wreck that it boiled over into my consciousness enough that I became fully aware and could begin the healing process.

As I healed, I developed more effective ways of managing the residual effects of the wreck. I began to live in full confidence. I began to change my line of questioning from "why me?" to "why not me?"

There's a reason that people watch and listen to me. There's a reason that complete strangers feel comfortable sharing their life stories with me. My brush with death allows me to connect the dots from a completely different perspective than the average person. I'm an encourager! I'm a bridge builder! I'm a creative problem solver! THIS IS MY PURPOSE! Every moment that I've been through has led me here, not for myself, but for other women! That's when I took my entrepreneurial journey to the next level by creating my business, Lindsey Vertner, LLC. As a personal development coach and speaker, I help women across the world know that they are worthy of genuine happiness in ALL areas of their lives.

Over the years, I noticed that women were struggling with these same issues. These beliefs may show up in their lives differently, but in the end, it always comes back to limiting beliefs around self-worth. I became intentional about helping friends with their self-worth struggles and noticed that their lives started to drastically improve. Just like me, they were trying to figure life out on their own. I became passionate about teaching other women how to break through their subconscious beliefs. I became passionate about teaching women how to get out of toxic relationships and create healthy boundaries. I became passionate about teaching women how to avoid becoming overwhelmed and burnout from the fifty different roles they juggle. I became passionate about teaching women that self-care is not selfish. I became passionate about teaching women how to find their own purpose and how to start creating the life of their dreams. I became passionate about speaking life into otherwise dead situations!

I want to speak to YOU directly. Your subconscious mind controls 95% of your behaviors. That means that until you identify the subconscious limiting beliefs that block you from your true desires, you will continue to run through the same cycles because you don't understand how those beliefs show up causing blocks in your life, your relationship, your career or business, your money, and more! You cannot heal what you are not aware of. Change starts with awareness. Once you are aware, then, you take action. You want results, and results come only from action. You do not have to be perfect. Progress is better than perfection. You can live a fulfilled life AND be a work-in-progress at the same time because limiting beliefs don't go away. You learn how to control them to work in your favor.

It's not by chance that you're reading these words! Stop doubting your worth. Know that you aren't just good enough, but YOU ARE MORE THAN GOOD ENOUGH! Psalm 139:14 states, "I praise you because I am fearfully and wonderfully made; your works are wonderful, I know that full well" (NIV).

You were created by God, and God's creations are wonderfully made! YOU ARE WONDERFULLY MADE! You are a QUEEN! You are a BOSS! And it's time for you to RISE!

Your potential is everything you have inside of you that you haven't done yet because you subconsciously believe that you aren't good enough. Allow me to teach you how to unlock that potential, step into your greatness, and live a passionate, fulfilled life! Book your *Unlock Your Greatness* session by sending an email to GetHappy@LindseyVertner.com.

Visit www.LindseyVertner.com for motivational content and to sign up for updates on my forthcoming book, *When Great Isn't Good Enough*. If you want to connect with myself and other likeminded women in person, sign up for live event updates at www.TheUnleashedWoman.net

The Queen Boss Rise

I am Enough

Tahira Best

https://www.facebook.com/illuminatedqueens

https:www.facebook.com/groups/illuminatedqueens

Website: https://www.tahirabest.com

Chapter 3

I am Enough

Tahira Best

I am a transformation coach who is passionate about helping my clients reawaken their desires, show up unapologetically and create a life so they love so they can show up as the Illuminated Queen they are meant to be. It has been a life-long journey arriving at my own path to self-actualization. My experiences have taught me to believe that women are much stronger than we realize. My story is one that brings this belief to life. Women have the power to achieve so much more than we currently do – especially when we are willing to share our vulnerability with others. I have learned that our stories unlock a prison door for somebody else and encourage them with the knowledge that they are not alone. With each trial and tribulation in life, I have learned that it's not how we get knocked down that determines who we are, but how we get back up. I now understand that the dark valleys of my life have proven to mold and shape me into the woman I have become. It's in these valleys that, we not only find out how much power we possess, but how much healing we still need to do.

My Trip to the Valley

I have always been the woman who wore her heart on her sleeve. I am a compassionate listener who loves helping people – at times to my own detriment. I am a family woman – family will always be number one for me. I am one who seeks to encourage people to discover their voice, especially those struggling in fear, because I know firsthand how terrifying it can be. Most of us are conditioned to think that vulnerability is a weakness that others can use to attack. I was raised by a strong, single black woman and I developed the same persona. I had to learn, that even though I am strong, all of us need support – we cannot be strong all of the time.

I even hid my vulnerability from my mother.

There was a point in my life that I hated who I was so much that I contemplated suicide. I felt like nothing I did was ever right and that I was not enough. I remember the day I sat on my couch, staring at a bottle pills – contemplating my death for about 20 mins. Obviously, I decided against it, not because I valued me as a person, but for my mom and family. I couldn't get rid of the image of my family at my funeral – and I knew that I couldn't do that to them. I kept hearing a voice telling me, "It's going to get better."

My journey from not valuing myself to falling head over heels in love with the woman I see in the mirror has made me passionate about making sure that all women know that they have a choice. As a child, I thought I was so cute. I was bold, loud, full of energy and my light shone bright and strong. For much of my childhood, I was bullied by little black girls, by the girls who looked just like me. They used to tell me that I spoke like a white girl and that I thought I was better than them. Whenever we got to recess, they would call me names, pull my hair, and push me off the swings and then call me "white girl." Maybe because I didn't use a lot of slang, and I absolutely loved pop and country music, to them, those things were what white girls did. It was like they just looked for opportunities to make my me feel bad, and each day my light shone a little less.

Over time, when I went to school, I didn't want to be noticed, so I was very quiet. I never wanted to stand out, so I blended in. I dimmed my light and I spent a lot of time questioning what was wrong with me. This nickname, "white girl," stuck with me all the way through high school and I constantly asked the question, "Am I black enough?"

In high school, things got a little better. We were all into boys, sports, and after school activities so there was less time to focus on a me. I found the one thing that I loved more than anything, which was cheerleading. It became my absolute passion and one of the only areas in my life where I felt happy and completely confident in my abilities. When I got to my junior year, we ended up getting a new coach, and having to adjust to the new methods was a little challenging.

During our competition season, my group had just had a really rough practice. Not only was one of my group members already injured, but my ankle was twisted, and I was limping all over the mat. After about an hour and a half of just fall after fall, we were all frustrated. We were the only group that day that was struggling and the more effort we gave, it felt like the worst it got. Eventually, the coach turned to our group, and yelled, "Why isn't it hitting? What's going on?" I responded, "I don't know."

She spent several minutes yelling about how we should be doing it and how we are not giving our all. I became angry and yelled back, "Then why don't you show me how to do it?" When it came out of my mouth, I knew I had messed up, so I began to walk out of the room to go to the bathroom and get myself together. I didn't want to say anything else disrespectful. When I started walking towards the door, she yelled, "Fine. Who needs you?" I turned around and yelled back, "I have been busting my ass for this team day in and day out and you would say something like that to me?" She told me, "Get out! Don't come back. We don't need you." I grabbed my stuff and left the room. I got to my car and cried before leaving.

I sat there thinking, "They don't need me. I was never good enough." I finally drove home and told me mom what had happened. She made me call and apologize. I was genuinely sorry. I didn't mean to yell at the coach, but my frustration throughout practice had just built up. After I apologized and explained myself, the coach let me know that she had already replaced me, finished explaining to me about the money that I owed the team, and that they wouldn't need me for the rest of the season. It hurt my soul and I decided in that moment, "I'm never giving my all again." Even when you give your all, you can make one mistake and lose everything. I just didn't feel good enough.

The Power of Words to Encourage

I finally went on to college and I thought, new people, new chances and an opportunity to reinvent myself. However, after months of trial and error in trying to adjust to my new life and after having another miscarriage, I fell into a depression. I no longer cared about school and I eventually failed out of college. I had a lot of thoughts while in the depression.

Am I good enough?

Am I smart enough?

Am I talented enough?

Am I woman enough?

I spent the next few weeks in a fog, just going through life. One day, I just decided that I needed a little getaway, so I got a hotel room and my plan was to just spend a few days by myself working through my anger, pain, frustration, and sadness. After hours of journaling, I called my boyfriend to come up and told him that I just needed a hug. When he got there, I just broke down in his arms and told how I just felt like no matter what I did or how hard I tried, it just was never enough. There was always something that felt unfinished, like I could have done more.

He looked at me and told me that he thought I was the most amazing woman he's ever met.

"You do everything for everyone, and at a moment's notice, whenever anyone has a problem, they call you because they know how good you are. They know how amazing you are. They know how special you are. We just want you to see you the way we all do."

I continued to cry, and I just melted in his arms, for what felt like hours. We woke up the next morning and he went to get us breakfast. I looked at some of the journal entries sitting on my desk and decided that was not going to be my present or future. I ripped them all up and threw them in the trash and decided to do better and be better every day.

The next day, I had a conversation with my mom about how I was struggling emotionally. She looked at me and said, "It's not how many times you get knocked down that matters, what matters most is how you get back up. Tahira, you can do anything that you put your mind to." She was right. I had thought of everything that I had to overcome to get to this moment. It didn't matter that I had problems in school. It didn't matter that I had made mistakes. What made this very moment possible is that I got back up.

The Climb Out of the Valley – You Can Change

I think it is important to share with you how I began to climb out of the valley. No matter where you are currently, you can emerge if you start with a plan and decide to act.

First, I realized that I had to fill my eyes with encouraging and motivating words. I started with affirmations – I posted a bunch of sticky notes everywhere in my home. Affirmations like, "I am strong. I am worthy of love and respect." I downloaded inspirational quotes on my phone so that I could see it when I opened and used my phone. I was very strategic about the music to which I was listening. I could no longer listen to love songs about exes and heartbreak.

Another thing I did was fill my mind with positive messages. I started reading books about mindset and personal development. Finally, I began to appreciate me. I started listing things that I liked about who I am. I spoke positive messages to myself, such as, "Tahira, you are beautiful in your own right. I love everything about you." During this phase, my mom stepped in again! She kind of forced me to look at what I was wearing. She pushed me to wear clothes more befitting. I started doing things that made me feel better instead of hiding my body – I started going to the gym and shopping, and I stopped isolating myself.

Now, some days it felt like it was unbearable, and it took me longer to get up, but what is most important is that I chose to get back up and I took steps every day. That is where my personal development journey began, and my passions eventually led me to a place where I help women move from pain to passion; they develop self-love, understand their worthiness, and unapologetically define and embrace their most authentic self.

Now I am Committed to…

This journey I have been on has been so rewarding and I am filled with gratitude. Benjamin Franklin said, "We must be happy with what we've got while we are in pursuit of what we want." I am committed to helping other women to experience the same gratitude from their own journey – enjoying and appreciating what life has already given.

I love to see transformation in my clients, witnessing their growth and owning who they are without worry of what other people think.

My journey has not been without fear. My biggest fear is the thought of doing this work, following my passion and getting to the end and failing. The thought of hearing all the naysayers saying, "I told you so." But I have learned to trust and believe in myself.

"Don't be disappointed if they can't see your vision because the blind can only see what they can touch"- Princess India Powell.

I repeat this quote to myself when I have doubts and fearful thoughts of what others think.

Tahira's final thoughts:

You must be willing, committed, and intentional about sacrificing who you used to be, to be reborn as the woman that you were meant to be. And yes, you can be fearful and courageous at the same time. Embrace the fact that it is possible to be afraid and courageous at the same time. You will rise up and embrace the authentic and unapologetic woman you need to be, both nervous and courageous as you stand up. Go after what you want and show up as the Queen Boss that you are.

The Queen Boss Rise

Emerge: Preparing to be Queen
Larkeia Matthews

Facebook: @uplevelme or Larkeia Matthews

email Larkeia.1Legacy@gmail.com

Linked In & Instagram: Larkeia Matthews

Chapter 4

Emerge: Preparing to be Queen

Larkeia Matthews

"Opportunities to find deeper powers within ourselves come when life seems most challenging." -- Joseph Campbell

Prepare for Vision

One day, you will realize that you have been preparing your whole life for the vision. Entrepreneurship doesn't start with the business creation; it all starts with a desire, a vision. In fact, vison is usually birthed from a desire to solve a problem in the world or to help improve upon the world and its people. The desire can be triggered in different ways, but often, life experiences and circumstances develop an interest or passion in us that otherwise would not have been. The magic is in the moment our interest and passion couples with our natural brilliance, then BOOM, our unique businesses can be born. We can start and build many empires, but the ones that will always excel are the ones that have a reason behind it that lies near to your heart. So, pray for the discernment to truly see the vision for your life and your business. Often, the two are closely connected and birthed from the same place.

The preparation for my vision was born out of traumatizing circumstances experienced in my childhood. Unfortunately, these circumstances didn't resolve in my youth. No, they created a variety of collateral damage that lingered and bled over into my adult life.

As a child, I watched my mother suffer from domestic violence at the hands of her spouse. Boom, Bam, then, loud cries rang in my ears. I silently agonized in my fear, frailty, and powerlessness. That was the sound of things breaking, being tossed and hitting the floor. I knew it would be a bad night when I heard arguing through the walls.

My biggest fear lay in the possibility of what could happen to her during those heated situations. My pain began with experiencing that someone that claims to love you could violate you and hurt you so tremendously. I was intently afraid to be a kid and be myself when my mother was not around because I never knew what exactly would land me in trouble. And his trouble terrified me. The minutest things were good enough for him to punish or physically whip me as if I weren't a small frail girl; which usually left my young body bruised and swollen.

He intimidated me into not revealing the details of my punishing to my mom, with the threat of being in more trouble. So, I made a choice to keep quiet, hoping she would intuitively discern his pattern and protect me.

I can't remember her and I ever speaking about what was going on in our home or how I was coping with it all; so, I grew accustomed to holding my emotions in with no safe space or hope for resolution. This began a toxic pattern. Losing hope at a young age created a cloud of darkness.

This created a toxic mixture brewing inside of me for years to come. I spiraled down a dark path of depression and developed a lot of hatred, most of which was directed at myself. I hated to be me and wished I was born someone else. I grew older not seeing value in who I was. By 17, I had run away twice, attempted suicide, and was dropping out of school. I believed that my future would be equally as painful my past and I wanted no part of that reality. By early adulthood, a lot had changed, but my mindset never really did.

I continued to attract toxic people and situations in my life and perpetuated cycles of struggle and pain. I searched for love in the wrong places, which connected me with people that added no value to me, but oh, did they did take. I stumbled around my life broken and with an emptiness. I went from thing to thing in search of something to help fill that void in my soul. It never did. I tried everything I knew, believing God would fix it for me one day. That day never came.

I was a functioning depressed woman, wife and mother by the end of my 20's. I had good times, but just as well at any given moment, tears could flow from my eyes due to my deep-seated discontentment with my life. I wanted more out of my life, but just didn't know how to get it. So, I began to really pray for lasting change, a real change. Well, have you ever heard the expression, "When a student is ready, a teacher will appear?" Well, that's what happened to me. I began to position myself to find a way to change my life for real. I searched and prayed continually. Little did I know; I was aligning myself with what I sought after.

One day, I was led to a woman who had the information that started the true beginning of my transformational journey. That day, things shifted in me and I was done being bruised and broken. At that point, my blinders came off and I truly saw and was disturbed by the effects my life was having on my kids. I wanted so much more and better for them! So, I decided to fight for my life and the possibility of a better one.

From that point on, I attached to my coach and immersed myself in the new knowledge of the power I had inside of me. I learned what I needed to do to heal and deprogram my current programing and learned how to reprogram myself with what I needed! I really went hard with reading and studying things like the mind and its powers, energy and metaphysics, how they play a part in how we are creating our lives. I studied spiritual laws, such as the Law of Attraction and the Law of Transmutation of Energy. I armed with all that information and I continued working on and learning about myself, rebuilding myself! Although I labeled it as work, because it is, it was hands down the best and most beneficial work I have ever done!

With a renewed perspective, I am convinced that everything I experienced thus far was merely preparation for my life's work and mission. I made it beyond depression, emptiness, and being stuck, to be of service to other women and teens. Yes, I had to develop a unique set of skills to make it from where I was to where I now am, but I did it and so can you! I've had to acquire new perspectives and mindsets and release old habits and beliefs. I've had to embrace healing and forgiveness like my life depended on it. I even had to identify mental and emotional blocks. The jumpstart for all progress for me was to learn to see myself for who I really am and to love me. I truly believe that so many of us could benefit tremendously from this teaching alone! Learning to cultivate that love, along with other self-development skills, will really put you in a new league! A Queen Boss League!

Prepare to Be Made Over

What is a Queen Boss? In honor of this book, I would like to share insight into these terms so that you may embrace its essence and own it in a new way! The dictionary says a Queen is someone that rules over a territory. I totally agree! I take it a step further; I say a Queen is one that rules over the territory of her mind and her life as only a Queen can. She asks no permission or needs no approval; she gives notice! She serves notice on her circumstances that they must alter themselves to fit her liking.

She decrees a thing to be and has the faith to expect it to be done! She clings to the scripture that says, "My word shall not return unto me void, it shall accomplish that in which I sent it!" (Isaiah 55:11). A Queen is not a victim; in fact, she took the power from being victimized and turned it in her favor. She understands that you cannot be a victim and victorious at the same damn time! So, she chooses victory hands down! I'm describing one powerful woman, in her presence and in her nature! Since this Queen had to take herself through periods of preparation to occupy that space, she can wear the crown!

Preparing the Mind

We were created divine by design with awesome power to create our lives in the fashion that we want it to be. In fact, we are always creating, even when we are not aware that we are. Awareness is one of the key elements in preparing to be Queen. We must become aware of the power of creation that we hold. When done correctly and intentionally, we can create ourselves and lives to be whatever we desire. I did! And am still doing it!

Your awareness is the activation key that unlocks everything else. Once you become aware of *what* you truly are, (Divine), then things begin to rearrange because your self-awareness and beliefs are now shifting!

This new alignment causes your actions to become more strategic and your mind will require new things from you. Push yourself. Lean into it. Don't give your allegiance to the familiar. Often, people hold on to who they have been while sacrificing who they can become! Don't! Learn to shift your mindset for the you that you have always known that you could be! Your best version of you deserves to come out and play!

A Queen Boss has a perspective that is unique and different from most of the world. You switch the programming in your mind to the channel that now resonates with your new awareness. For example, she sees opportunity when others see scarcity, and lessons where others see defeat!

Not matter if a glass is half empty or full, the Queen learns to picture it overflowing! With this type of renewed mind, you are prepared you to be your own hero!

You can then start to make decrees over your life. You can use your words as your staff and wield it in the direction you want your life to go. Although things may not happen directly when you speak, this is where the strengthening of your faith comes in to play.

You must seek to fortify your mind to be not easily broken. Let's not forget to allow time for things to take shape. It will when you are in alignment! Just don't abort the process. You are worth the wait! There are always going to be trying times but giving in to them will only increase their intensity and duration. It is normal to feel the emotions, but implore resiliency to say, "*Okay now, let's get back on track and press through.*"

Weave and craft such strength into your character that you meet adversity head on and win. I've taken many blows while on my transformational journey and learned that I can bend but not break!

Prepare your Spirit

Anything is possible to him that believes! Winners are willing to step out on faith beyond what they can see with the willingness to walk alone. When you are aligned with your creator, your source, being in awe of its power, faith becomes a natural knowing! In this identity, you must possess that same element of faith, in yourself, accompanied by confidence. When you are feeling with your heart and allowing yourself to be led, you can naturally craft a type of confidence that is felt without you having to say a word.

This takes time and dedication to become part of the natural fabric that makes up YOU. But, as I said before, this is a necessary part of the journey to be that Boss you know you can and should be!

When preparation meets determination, you will be able to cast a vision so powerful that it leaves an imprint on the world. I let my pain lead me to a passion to Heal, Equip, and Empower. That is what the H.E.R stands for in my Business name which is, *HER Legacy Inspires.* I coupled that with my unique gifts of teaching, writing, and discernment to create a service! I use my gifting to see into another's struggle and identify where the core issue lies, then implore expertise to map out a plan and walk with them down the path to freedom and victory.

If something in my story triggered a desire in you to want assistance to go to another level in your possibility, I urge you to reach out to me! *HER Legacy* is here for you, built for you. Don't allow your doubt to keep you in a box trying to do it alone. That was never God's Plan. We need one another! Remember my story. I tried it alone, but when I asked for help and was ready to receive it, my teacher appeared, and I never looked back! Keep in mind unprocessed emotions and an untamed mind can and will be huge success blockers. Queens don't block; they position themselves for success! For every Queen that is ready to get assistance on her Journey to the next level, I have something to offer you for purchasing this awesome book and being willing to invest in yourself. You will get a complimentary 60-minute BreakThrough session with me, CEO of *HER Legacy Inspires* currently valued at $139.

YESS! I get so excited about the come up of other Queens! Check my bio for my contact information and send me an email with the book title in the subject line and the words 'Ready to emerge' in the body. Get ready to create a new mind-blowing story called your life! Queens Rise!

The Queen Boss Rise

Hope Found in the Scars

Ayingi Kimble

ayinlifeministries@gmail.com
Instagram-ayingikimble
Facebook Ayingi Kimble
Linkedin Ayingi Kimble
Facebook Ayin Life Ministries
Grow & Glow Podcast @ The Provoke Factor
Grow & Glow Podcast @Provoke Magazine Media

Chapter 5

Hope Found in the Scars

Ayingi Kimble

Early Glimpses of My Calling

I have always been the person who family members come to with their problems and issues. From a very young age, I was good at explaining and deciphering their feelings – helping them to see from the viewpoint of the other person. I thought it was normal, then years later, I realized that not everyone had this gift.

I think it all began that fateful morning of my childhood that would scar the rest of my life. That was the day that I went to bed a little girl and woke up a mother of three. I had to step into the role of mother, protector, nurturer, and caregiver.

...more about this later.

I am a transformational life-coach. I have recognized the "good in all things" including my deepest scars and share them to inspire others to thrive. As a speaker, author, and transformational coach, I host workshops that encourage attendees to feel the pain, embrace the scars and patch together the scraps of their lives and begin the process of healing, recognizing that the scars are beautiful badges of honor from the past to be used as fuel for the future.

The Tale of Two Mornings

One morning, I woke up late, anxious that I had not made breakfast for my 14-year-old daughter. As I jumped up in the bed, frantic to care for her as I had all of her life, she was headed out the door, waving back at me, "Bye mom. I already made breakfast. I love you." In that moment, I thought, Oh My God, she will be graduating high school in two years. What am I going to do with myself? I was catapulted back to when I was 9 years old.

That morning, I did not smell my breakfast cooking, so I went out on the veranda looking for my mother. She was not in the kitchen, so I continued my search. As I walked out back, I was horrified to find her hanging from a swing in our back yard. My mind raced, connecting the two mornings.

I immediately realized how I had been using my daughter as a crutch to ignore my mother's death. I had made excuses for years about how I could not move forward with my life because I had a young daughter for which to care. I was 16 years old when I gave birth to her and I felt as if people began to assume that my life was finished, thinking that I would continue to have babies and never do much else with my life. It is funny how the mind works – connecting our thoughts and memories over time and space.

That morning, as my daughter walked out the door, my emotional crutch was removed, and it forced me to look at myself. I knew that if my life was to change, I must go back to the event that first changed me – that moment when I was no longer the happy little girl chasing high grades. I grew up immediately and my life changed forever. Because of the experience of losing my mother to suicide, I was stuck in a cycle of pain for over two decades.

Facing the Scars - Dealing with the Past and Living in the Present

At the age of 29, I was faced with the realization that I needed to work through my mom's death emotionally. Because suicide is a subject about which most people are not comfortable talking, it was and still is taboo in our culture. I never again talked about my mother. It was as if she had never existed - I didn't cry, I didn't talk about it, and I didn't grieve (outwardly that is). I spent over two decades suppressing the memories and hiding my grief and feelings of abandonment and rejection with anger. I now know that buried emotions never die; they only resurface in other areas. What I had suppressed played out in all my relationships and everything I did – even in the workplace. Once I decided that I needed to face that chapter in my life that changed me, I knew what I had to do. This meant I would need to speak up, cry and lay all my cards on the table so I could get to the place of inner peace that I once thought was not attainable. I joined and completed an eight-week counseling program in Jamaica called, *Getting Past your Past* at Choose Life International, which specializes in suicide prevention. Through this program, I accepted my part in nurturing this pain as well as my role in the negative experiences I had encountered in my life. I was able to ask family members questions and get some insight into who my mom was and what contributed to her abrupt ending. I was able to finally experience closure. I was finally able to go to my mother's grave.

Hope Breathed New Life – The Power of My Own Voice

For the first time in my life, I had hope. I was able to wholeheartedly accept all of me, scars and all. It was like a weight was lifted off my shoulders and new air was disbursed into every fiber of my being. I started to smile with the world and experience the world smiling back at me. I was able to give love and accept love. This is when I met my husband and how I ended up moving to the United States.

I came to understand the power of my voice and the impact my testimony had on others when I started to accept radio and television interviews while I still lived in Jamaica. Three years later I started working at Choose Life International and realized my purpose and natural gift in helping people heal from trauma, pain or loss and navigate life's journey. I then got an inside peek into some of the feelings my mom might have harbored. My life experiences have sharpened my gift of insight for those who are hurting, as I connect with them on an emotional level. My clients are people who have had a loss, remain stuck and have not given themselves the chance to grieve. It could be the loss of a relationship, a job, a friendship or losing a loved one suddenly. The person who is a rebel but unsure of their cause lives in chronic loneliness and always feels victimized. This client is who I describe as going through the "common denominator effect" but is unaware of their part or why the cycle seems to "follow them."

Now I am Committed to...

My motivation now is to see loss survivors experience freedom and not just survive but thrive -no longer carrying the weight of their experiences.

I exemplify the transformation one can achieve after they decide to grab life by the horns and push through the innate and unexplained guilt, shame, and unworthiness they experience after feeling abandoned and rejected by a loved one. I no longer live with the need to please and seek out my value by over serving those around me. I understand and accept that I am a child of God and loved by my Creator. I now live in a constant state of gratitude, no matter what comes my way. I understand my response to life's challenges will always direct the outcome that I experience in life. Life is not happening to us; our responses change everything.

The fact that I can smile from a place of inner glow challenges how people choose to exist while they are on this earth. I exemplify a woman of fortitude who chose determination over inner devastation by not letting the pressures of life overcome me. The impact I aspire to create will help to heal generations to come. I intend to stir a shift in others that will get them to research the spiritual heritage they are living, empowering them to break the family pathologies of dysfunctions - one person at a time, leading the way for those coming behind them.

I have been able to share my voice, dramatically impacting those people who need to hear my message. One young woman who saw one of my interviews was prompted to call in and seek help as she was planning to take her own life. She, like my mom had four children and was only twenty- seven years old. As I spoke, I was able to relate to her pain by baring my own scars, giving her insight into how her choices would scar her children for life. She expressed gratitude to me for speaking and explained that seeing me made her see that she did not want to leave her children with that kind of pain. From my story and my work with her, she started to dream again after we identified beliefs that were holding her back. She found strength to walk away from unhealthy relationships and went back to training school. She then got a job and was able to care for her children on her own terms.

My clients experience release and relief from the trap of unforgiveness. My clients experience better days as they undergo massive attitude shifts, helping them to accept responsibility for their own life experiences – and now have revived faith. My clients are able to hold up their mirror of truth without shame and guilt and see love, purpose, triumph, victory, and a deep appreciation of their own life's journey.

Steps to Move from Surviving to Thriving

❖ ***Recognize Your Own Natural Gifts***: There are things that I do with little to no effort because they are gifts. I am empathic with interpersonal gifts that allow me to relate to someone whom I have never met. I used unconsciously fear compliments and recognitions. I have now learned to embrace them.

❖ ***Choose to be Free and Serve on your Own Terms***: Freedom to me means that I get to create my schedule. I can serve from anywhere in the world, if I have my computer and a good Wi-Fi signal. I can decide if and when I want to work, and I am able to travel to see other parts of the world.

❖ ***Remember That Failing Is Not the End of The World***: It is the catalyst that pushes us forward and lets us know what works and what does not work for me, my mission and the people I serve.

❖ ***Learn How to Get Out of Your Own Way and Ask for Help***: Reach out to those around you. Once I did this, none of the mountains seemed quite as high as I thought they were.

❖ ***Learn to Master Your Thoughts***: One fear that manifested was the Imposter Syndrome. In my case, this was the fear of not being good enough as I scrolled social platforms and started the comparison conversation in my own head.

❖ *Take Things One Step at a Time* As women, we like a road map of where we are going as this makes us feel secure. I have learned to focus on one task at a time and celebrate micro wins along the way.

❖ *It Is OKAY to Not Have It All Figured Out.* Admit it, ask for help, or just take a break from it all and do a fun activity in order to recharge.

❖ *Start by Writing Your Vision Down or Create A Vision Board of All the Things You Want to Accomplish.* Then go for it, as a thousand miles begins by taking one step at a time.

The fact that you are reading this book means you already have a desire to make your mark in this world by starting a business that God has placed in your heart.

Being a Queen Boss requires getting in the ring in order to make you mark, take a punch or be able to give a punch. Just like in boxing, one must be in the ring. Brené Brown says it this way, "If you are not in the arena also getting your ass kicked, I am not interested in your feedback." It requires childlike faith in order to persevere.

I can be reached at ayinlifeministries@gmail.com

Instagram-ayingikimble,

Facebook Ayingi Kimble,

Linkedin Ayingi Kimble,

Facebook Ayin Life Ministries;

Grow & Glow Podcast @ The Provoke Factor

Grow & Glow Podcast @Provoke Magazine Media

After the Storm

Jacinta Paris

Social Media:

IG: @lovelifevirtualsolutions

FB: facebook.com/lovelifevirtualsolutions

Website: lovelifevirtualsolutions.com

🌿 Chapter 6

After the Storm

Jacinta Paris

It started back in 2013; that was a monumental year for me. I had accomplished one of the biggest achievements of my life. All the hard work, resilience, sweat and tears of a dream I had since I was 11 years old had been realized. I had finally gotten my Bachelor of Arts degree in Communications from the University of North Carolina at Charlotte. I was on top of the world (or so it would seem to everyone else). I remember that day like it was yesterday. I stood with thousands of other graduates and accepted my diploma. It was a job well done! My parents were so proud. All the money, energy, and time they had invested in me for so many years led up to that one day. Even while achieving that esteemed accomplishment, something inside just didn't feel quite right.

I went on to get a job in my field that year working for a reputable radio station, and "on paper," I was doing everything my parents, society, and popular culture says you should be doing at that stage in life. On paper, I should've been happy. On paper, I was everything that a parent, daughter, sister, or friend should want. Inside, I was miserable. I felt unfilled. I honestly felt like a complete failure. For the next year and a half, I spent my time bouncing from job to job. I worked for a reputable radio station, went on to work in the admissions department at a college, and then a sales company. I was searching for purpose - I was searching for identity.

I didn't want to get lost in the sea of corporations; I wanted to be successful and enjoy what I did for a living. I knew the job I had at the time or any of the jobs I had done at that point was going to do that for me. I would spend my own work shift with a journal just creating, and brainstorming ideas of this dream empire I wanted to build. I envisioned myself having the freedom to travel as much as I wanted, make as much money as I wanted, while making an impact in the lives of others in the process. At the time, I had no idea where I was going with all the emotions I was feeling or the ideas I would write about. All I knew was that I wanted more, needed more.

Building a Dream Empire on Sand

One day after work, one of my close friends invited me to dinner. She had had a rough week at work and needed someone to vent to. We hadn't spoken in a while, so we caught up and began updating one other on what was going on in life. It didn't take much time to realize that we both shared the same feelings about life, our careers, and lack of fulfillment. We were tired of going to work every single day to a job we hated, making less than we knew we both deserved. It felt so refreshing to finally talk to someone who was going through what I was going through and feeling the same way I was feeling.

We put our heads together and started brainstorming solutions, and that night, *Paramount Cleaners* was born. For the next two months, we worked relentlessly to get our business off the ground. We did countless hours of research, established a brand name, filed business documents, studied the systems and structures of successful cleaning companies, designed our own website/marketing materials, researched the absolute best cleaning products to use, and started advertising. Within the first few days of our business launch, we landed our first customer and the rest was history. It was the best feeling ever!

Our business started taking off shortly after and within three months, we had gotten so busy we were able to quit our jobs. We were so ecstatic! We no longer had to commute to jobs we hated; we had the freedom to create our daily schedules, write our own paychecks, and choose our clients. Everything was perfect, and for the first time in a very long time, we were content with life and the direction we were going. Business was booming, and our phones were ringing constantly with requests for service. We felt such great senses of purpose and achievement. We felt like we had finally accomplished the "dream".

Ignoring the Signs

In the midst of living our dream, we began to get overwhelmed and burnt out QUICKLY. We thought pushing ourselves to the limit working 13-18 hours a day, would ultimately be the key to our success, but in reality, we were overworking ourselves. We thought handling all aspects of the business meant more money in our pockets, less we would have to kick out, and more money we could use to reinvest into the business. Instead of focusing on our individual talents and maximizing our skills in the areas we were the strongest, we thought we could do it all. Little did we know, that was a recipe for disaster. We were going about things the wrong way.

People don't talk about all the depression, stress, anxiety, and overwhelm that comes with entrepreneurship. Entrepreneurs are four times more likely to suffer from depression and 30% of entrepreneurs experience depression in some form over the course of their careers. It can be one big roller coaster of emotions. The financial stresses, the desire to want to overachieve and in the beginning, the feeling of not being where you truly want to be. All of these emotions combined can really propel you into a state of distress and hopelessness, especially if you aren't already emotionally stable.

We started feeling every bit of that wave. We were feeling the weight of the world on our shoulders. We were working harder instead of smarter and we had no clear vision for our business. We knew we wanted to be "Successful," but somewhere along the way, we lost sight of what our definition of success was. We had no back-end support or real guidance, and we were exhausting ourselves with every element of the business.

I was what people would call a "high functioning depressive," but the effects that it had on my friend were devastating. Her personality started to change, and she just wasn't herself anymore. I could see the toll it was taking on the both of us, but especially her. She was losing herself. She came to me one day and said, "Jacinta, I can't do this anymore. I have to take a step back to figure this all out."

The Walls Came Crashing Down

Once she left the business, I took on things full time. The stresses of the daily operations got even more frustrating. It became hard for me to manage everything, and over the course of the next year, I experienced business financial woes, depression, severe anxiety, suicidal thoughts and an unexpected seizure. I had no direction and I felt like I had nowhere to turn. I was at my absolute lowest point, and for the first time, I started questioning why I even left my job in corporate America. I began to see first-hand how "anti" glamorous entrepreneurship really was.

December 27, 2017. It's a day I will never, ever forget. I got up as usual and began doing things to start my day. I had a weird feeling in my spirit that whole morning, and I couldn't quite put my finger on it. It was like a dark cloud was over my head. Around 11:30 am, QBR, I got a phone call that broke my heart into a million pieces. My friend and former business partner had committed suicide. My heart instantly fell into my chest. I was devastated. I just remember feeling a million different negative emotions at once. I started thinking about all the things I had tried to do to save her - none of that mattered in that moment. She was gone.

I sank into a deep, dark depression, and for a straight month, there wasn't a day that went by that I didn't cry. I did everything to pull myself out of that rut, but nothing was working. I began going back to the source and what had been my foundation for so long. I started praying to God asking him for a way out. I started asking God for peace and guidance.

Picking up the Pieces

One day, I was doing some research online and I got a message from someone who said he was a Virtual Assistant. He started explaining all the ways he could help save some time and money in my business. At first, I was very reluctant because I had never heard of a Virtual Assistant, but being the curious person that I am, I started doing research. I remember thinking to myself, "Wow, why didn't I run across someone like this sooner?" I purchased two weeks' worth of his services and I remember beginning to see the light at the end of the tunnel. Suddenly, all my anxiety, stress, and overwhelm of the business began to prune.

After doing some serious soul searching, I decided to let the cleaning business go and really go after what God had put on my heart to pursue the entire time.

I started *Love Life Virtual Solutions* for the burnt out/overwhelmed female entrepreneurs that lack balance and back end support in their businesses. *Love Life Virtual Solutions* is a virtual support company that provides general administration, social media, lifestyle, and event management to clients. We also just launched an online shop with office items and accessories that can go in a woman's office space. My sole mission is to give clients a sense of balance in their professional lives and save them more time and energy to focus on their growing empire.

Starting *Love Life Virtual Solutions* has really changed my outlook on life, and entrepreneurship; it has given me a clear sense of purpose. I get to work hand in hand with my clients to help them grow their business, and I get to support them every step of the way. I have the financial freedom to work wherever I want, whenever I want and with whoever I want to work with. I've been able to travel more than I've ever traveled before, and I have some amazing clients. My brand gives me a sense of fulfillment and purpose that I've never had before.

I miss my friend so much and there's not a day that goes by that I don't think of her. I think about all the things we said we would achieve. We prayed so hard for those things. She would be so proud. My life has literally become the product of those prayers and I'm so thankful for that.

For the longest, I use to envy people who seemed to have life all figured out and always knew exactly what they wanted to be and how they planned to get there. It was never that simple for me. I had to go through some major storms and fight through some painful moments to get to my path of purpose. Sometimes, our purpose in life isn't always crystal clear. Sometimes, God will allow us to take a dark and painful route just so that he can lead us back to the path that we are destined to be on all along. During that storm, you have to be strong enough to fight through and know that what you're going through has divine purpose even if you don't understand it.

In Loving Memory of my Dear Friend. Gone, But Never, Ever Forgotten.

Social Media:

IG: @lovelifevirtualsolutions

FB: facebook.com/lovelifevirtualsolutions

Website: lovelifevirtualsolutions.com

Releasing the Weight

Tiffany Williams

Website: www.phoenixfitfans.com (Under Construction)

Facebook business page:

https://www.facebook.com/PFFCoachIT/

Instagram:
https://www.instagram.com/phoenixfitnessfanaticscoachit/

Chapter 7

Releasing the Weight

Tiffany Williams

When I first started personal training, I didn't see it as a service that I could provide. I saw it as me simply sharing what I did to drop the weight I had recently lost with my friends and family members. When my journey began, I weighed nearly 300 pounds and was determined to do everything I could to get healthy. (That is an entire book in itself, but for another time). As I succeeded in releasing weight, I had many people asking me the secret to my success. To me, it wasn't a secret. I was just another unhealthy, chunky girl working out in the gym trying to get healthy…that's it.

In addition to focusing on releasing weight, I soon became interested in feeding my mind to assist with my weight release. I even changed the way I addressed losing weight. I started saying I was, "releasing weight," not "losing it." Someone once told me when you refer to losing something you always have the possibility of finding it, but when you release something, you can release it for good.

I also read books with a positive vibe like, *The Secret*, by Rhonda Byrne or *Abundance Now*, by Lisa Nichols. My collection still grows to this day. All these books influenced my thinking about how I needed to share my story and the knowledge I had learned. I released 118.7 pounds and people needed to know how I did it. I started out by calling my friends when I'd go work out and I'd include them in the workout routine or have them meet me at the park to walk.

Sharing the Journey

After seeing continued success in my own journey, my "why" became my need to satisfy the desire I had to help women find hope and support. I didn't want anyone to feel lost like I did because, we as the leaders in our jobs, homes, and communities, tend to lose ourselves to the endless hours of chaos in our lives. We neglect to fill our own cup and run on empty, forgetting how it feels to be healthy until it's too late.

Growing up, I was always taught not to talk to people or share my thoughts with them, because either they were being nosey or just trying to get into my business. I was scolded for wanting to converse with people, but to me that's what makes us human. Today, I've learned that sharing ones struggles and revealing the things you have accomplished through your journey is an amazing tool that can change another person's life! When you have successfully conquered a hill someone else is struggling to climb, you must share your trials and tribulations that got you up that hill. The share inspires others to start their own climb.

My Story the Bridge to My Clients

I have attracted quite a few women who are feeling tired and frustrated with the ups and downs of losing weight and always finding it again. They are lost and often just trying to find the right combination of what to eat, how to get started in the gym, and even how to properly provide themselves with the level of self-care (which is a necessity in this journey.) They hate the word "diet," and feel trapped because they can't seem to get out of the crazy weight gain cycle leading them right back to their unhealthy state again.

Some of my clients are stuck in broken relationships because they don't think they matter enough to break free from the toxic environments or don't think they deserve anything better. When I step in to work with my clients, I help them recognize their worth again and to take care of the valuable person that they are. One of my clients once called me her "Flashlight." She said I was brought into her life to bring her out of the darkness. I Just LOVE being that light! My clients learn how to release weight and keep it off for good. They learn to ignite that inner fire, so they can release desired weight, feel better about themselves, create a more balanced healthy home for their families, feel more energetic and less joint pain, and best of all, they could potentially regulate some serious health issues just by following my lead.

My Story, My Passion, My Business

For me, releasing the weight was the easiest part when I decided to focus on opening a business surrounding my love of fitness and my success of dropping 118.7 pounds for good. Everything seemed so complicated from opening a business account to creating my social media pages such as a Facebook group page, Instagram and LinkedIn pages as well.

In the beginning, I really didn't think I had a story or that my journey of releasing that much weight didn't matter. It wasn't until I started discovering various Facebook Groups with growing women entrepreneurs telling their amazing stories, that I realized, "My story did matter!" At that point, I came across a video of a Business Coach who caught my eye. She wasn't gimmicky, and I liked that she seemed real. The video was about charging what you are worth. It was so clear; I was not at all charging what my services were worth. While I still find it a challenge to charge a higher price, I know they are worth every penny!

The rewards my clients receive by following my lead are priceless. When I think about it, the knowledge provided could potentially add years to someone's life. Once, a co-worker looked discouraged. I asked what was wrong and she said that she was recently diagnosed as pre-diabetic. After applying some of my weight release tips, she came back to see me a couple of days after her 90-day check up with her doctor. She was no longer pre-diabetic! A few of my VIP clients have been able to fit into clothes they haven't been able to fit in for years. To see their face light up brings me complete joy!

Overcoming my Own Mindset Blocks

When I attempted to start my business, I didn't feel like I was worthy to give advice without the educational background along with all the certifications. After working with a few individuals and talking to some professionals in the industry, I realized that I was giving away my services which could hurt me. So, it's not always about the credentials you have. I had to remember that other Coaches all started somewhere just like me, and surprisingly, most of them started out without credentials and grew into their roles as leading Fitness Professionals in the industry. They taught me that by not charging people, they did not see me as their Health/Fitness Coach. I was just their friend working out with them in the gym, park, or in some cases, my living room., which was right. When I got out of my own head and started charging, my events started to grow. My friends started inviting their friends and before long, they were almost double in size. Instead of having 2 or 3 friends it was 6 or 7. When you believe in yourself and what you have to offer, people will also believe in the product or service you have to offer.

Show people your product or service is the best one for them and that you are the solution to their problem!

BELIEVE IN YOURSELF AND SET YOUR INTENTIONS!

One last thing I want to share with you about growing my business is, you can't be a perfectionist. Things are going to go wrong; people are going to say no. You just need to keep on pushing! Things don't always have to be perfect and all you really need to do is show up, share your brilliance with the world, and you will make an impact. When you believe in yourself and your abilities, you can change lives!

In the past year, surrounding myself with like-minded and driven women, realizing I am not alone in this, and hiring a phenomenal Business Coach, helped to develop the confidence and determination I needed to rise as a Queen Boss. Get ready world!!

Next year, I am proud to announce I will be launching my Virtual Fitness Training programs and I will be hosting the "Sundays at Tiffany's" meal prep series on YouTube. We are also working on opening a local gym location in Southern California that will focus on nurturing and developing children's talents while providing busy parents a place to unwind as they get in a good workout, enjoy great company, awesome music, and so much more!

Through my journey to become an Entrepreneur, I have met some very strong, brilliant women who have inspired me to stretch myself to my limits. They have made me feel uncomfortable at times in conversations, mad when calling me out for not putting in the work I promised, but they have also become my sisters. These women are my, "Sherries," real women slaying their dreams and goals left and right! A Queen Boss at her finest! These women shine bright in the world. They are amazing in their area of expertise. They handle their homes and businesses like a champ but never forget to make time for important things like quality family time and self-care.

As my business continues to thrive and grow, I aspire to be the best Queen Boss I can and look forward to sharing my whole story with you. Until next time…Stay Bossy Queen!

Business Name: Phoenix Fitness Fanatics

Website: www.phoenixfitfans.com (Under Construction)

Facebook business page:

https://www.facebook.com/PFFCoachIT/

Instagram:
https://www.instagram.com/phoenixfitnessfanaticscoachit/

Don't Count Me Out
Sabrina Thomas

Website: www.sabrinatspeaks.com
Facebook & Instagram: @SabrinaTSpeaks
Facebook & Instagram: @SabrinaTheIEPCoach
Email: sabrinatspeaks@gmail.com sabrinatheiepcoach@gmail.com

Chapter 8

Don't Count Me Out

Sabrina Thomas

"Until you have a kid with special needs you have no idea of the depth of your strength, tenacity and resourcefulness."

~Anonymous

I am a Queen Boss

I am a coach, an author, proud mother of two sons, one with special needs. I am a fierce advocate for him and the families who embrace a child with special needs. A few years ago, I decided I also wanted to become an entrepreneur. Entrepreneurship comes with its fair share of challenges, but I have absolutely no regrets. It is not something I would trade for anything in this world. As a speaker, coach, and advocate, I can live out my passion. I aspire to do more with the special-needs community on a global scale. Through the day-to-day struggles of entrepreneurship, I have gained the strength and courage to go after my vision with my God-given purpose in mind. In my eyes, I already see myself as being a Queen Boss. In my opinion, this is a female who is highly driven, fierce, outspoken and one who gets the job done. It doesn't matter whether it is to be a homemaker, a stay at home mom, a working mom or a mom-preneur. The bottom line is this: Queen bosses have a goal in mind, and they work to ensure that this goal is accomplished while balancing everything else.

You Can't See through Muddy Water – that Doesn't Mean the Fish Aren't There

My entrepreneurial journey has not been an easy one and has its own share of rewards and challenges. From the beginning, I had challenges that ranged from gaining visibility, making my presence known in social media, technology difficulties, and of course, my personal responsibilities of caring for my family. As I build my business, I am working part time and still in transition to full entrepreneurship. I often struggle with finding the time to take care of everything and still have time for myself. As I dealt with and overcame those challenges, I found the reward of running my own business. It is something that I personally created – made from the muddy situations that life gave me. I am determined to leave a legacy for my children and other children and families with special needs. I know that the work I am doing is not short term and will go on to make a positive impact for generations to come.

I have had to deal with the fear of failing – yes, fear does creep in. I feared that no one would take me seriously and consider me a successful entrepreneur – making a difference in this world. I found that it comes with a change in one's mindset and true change comes from within. As I changed on the inside, my life started to shift.

Global Vision

Starting entrepreneurship takes dedication to remain in the struggle. While I have made an impact, I look forward to making global impact within the special-needs community. I may not know all the answers, but I will find them. My main goal is to provide support any way it is needed. I aspire to do more with the special-needs community on a global scale and I seek to make connections when and wherever I can to get this message to the world.

The Cold, Hard Truth

My Son, Omar, was diagnosed with cerebral palsy when he was two and a half years old and later with an intellectual disability and autism. Though I didn't know it at the time, I began the grieving process at the age of thirty-three, at the time of the first diagnosis, and I continued to grieve each year and with each diagnosis. I still remember the day that the doctor delivered the news. Though I knew that my son was developmentally delayed, nothing could have prepared me for that cold and final diagnosis. The school had referred me to have Omar tested for the intellectual disability diagnosis and I was sent to several specialists for a variety of tests. That was mentally exhausting in itself, but when the results came back, I was taken aback by the cold delivery of the diagnosis – with a pat on the back and a pamphlet. I left the doctor's office stunned, not knowing my next steps.

To say that I was hurt, angry, and alone is an understatement. Fear, shame, guilt and extreme sadness fell quickly on my shoulders and consumed me. Suddenly, the child that I thought I had was no longer. Everything I planned for my son was gone and I was devastated. The fear of the unknown almost paralyzed me as I thought of raising a child who could not communicate his needs. That realization has been the hardest for me – I had to learn how to discern when he is in pain, paying close attention to Omar so that I could properly care for him. That is how my journey began as an advocate for families of disabled children.

After the Pity Party is Over – School was About to be In-Session

After I had a pity party for a while, wallowing in "what could have been" for my son, I woke up one morning realizing that my self-pity would get me nowhere quickly. I knew that I had work to do. I started researching everything I could about Omar's disabilities. I devoured any reading I could find – scouring the internet and picking the brains of anyone who could assist me. Taking "no" for an answer was not even an option. I started educating myself and I quickly gathered the knowledge I needed to be an advocate for others as well. I attended meetings and conferences to educate myself. I met new people and began to connect and network with other like-minded entrepreneurs as well. This began to lift my spirits as I recognized that there are so many people suffering and grieving the same way I was. I was no longer suffering in isolation. There are so many people suffering and grieving the same way I was. I was no longer suffering in isolation.

Initially, I wanted to become an entrepreneur so that I could be there for Omar to support him. However, along the journey, it became more than just wanting to be there. I found that I really enjoyed what

I was doing because I was working to build leaders and empower families. My focus became about educating families and caregivers on how they can become better advocates for their children. I wanted to empower others by sharing with them my personal experience as a parent of a son with special needs. As a result, I have become a speaker, advocate, author, and coach.

The Toll it Takes on the Family is Tremendous

Because I have been where they are, I know what it's like to have everything revolve around your child's needs to the point that the other members in the family suffer. I know the toll it can take both mentally and physically on the parent or caregiver personally. You are often left feeling as though the weight is just too much to bear. There are times that you just want to know that there is someone out there who understands exactly through what you are going. It doesn't matter if you are a single parent or married, it can be completely overwhelming. Oftentimes, we neglect other members in the family as we work to address the needs of the one disabled.

Out of the Shadows and into the Light

Through working with my son, I found my love for advocacy. Often feeling alone and that no one understood what I was going through, I wanted to become that woman that I needed for mothers now. Through my son's disability, I found my passion and purpose and in turn, it has given me the opportunity to care for him effectively while empowering others to do the same for their children. My biggest inspiration is my son. The time I spend with him teaches me lessons every day that I look forward to sharing with others.

Now I am Committed to…

My business is here for you to feel empowered as the best possible advocate you can be. I take a lot of pride in what I do daily and love when my clients and parents feel satisfied with the services I provide. I believe it is our responsibility as parents to be a voice for our children who can't speak for themselves. I am the voice for my clients until they can speak. I want my clients and their children to know that they are not alone. We are all on this journey together and I am here to provide any support they may need. I encourage families to know, that no matter what the child's needs are, they are strong and equipped enough to handle it.

A goal of mine is to teach the importance of self-growth through the process. I let my clients know that they should not lose themselves in the process. By making yourself a priority, you are also helping your child to feel empowered. Their well-being is very important, but so is yours. I let them know that their livelihood, happiness, and leadership skills can't exist unless they take the time to care for themselves. Remember, how you care for your-well-being as you care for your child, they will pick up that energy. My clients are equipped, educated and empowered to be their child's best caretaker and advocate.

Tips for Recognizing the Opportunities Hidden in the Obligations

I would like to caution women looking to begin your entrepreneurial journey - to recognize your current job as a blessing. Your current job is not some dead weight holding you back and stopping you from achieving your full potential. Instead, it is the gasoline that will keep your entrepreneurial journey alive. Without the steady paycheck, you would be spending all your time trying to raise money rather than spending your time investing and perfecting your business. Do not think of your job as something that is dragging you down, but rather as your partner who is giving you that support you need until it is time for you to separate. One of the major disadvantages of a job is that you need to invest at least 40 hours each week working on something that is not your main priority. Learn to maximize your time. There are 168 hours in each week, your job takes 40, your sleep takes 56 and you are left with all of 72 hours to build your business. Make a schedule and plan time accordingly. I know that you might say that you have obligations and I get that. I get that you need food and you may have children and outside responsibilities. I am also encouraging you to see the opportunities available right in the midst of those obligations.

Do what you can and outsource whatever you are not able to do personally. You will find you can get a lot done; it is all about arranging and making the most of every day. Draft a timeline, decide what you can do and what you can't, then take it from there. Initially, when I started, I had a goal, a focus of where I wanted to be. I have accomplished some of that, but I have more to do.

At the core of my business is impact. One might think that when their business reaches a certain stage of growth and stability, that is the time to make an impact. That stage might be too late, so don't wait. Strive to make an impact from conception. Very early in my business, I made giving and helping others a key part of our purpose. If your initial focus was to have an impact, you will find that every day you make a difference in someone's life. You too can be a Queen Boss!

Sabrina Thomas

www.sabrinatspeaks.com

Facebook & Instagram: @SabrinaTSpeaks

Facebook & Instagram: @SabrinaTheIEPCoach

Email: sabrinatspeaks@gmail.com sabrinatheiepcoach@gmail.com

Finding the Right Fit to Soar

Morgan Edwards

Website: www.yourchieftechofficer.com

Email: hello@yourchieftechofficer.com

Facebook: www.facebook.com/yourchieftechofficer.com

Chapter 9

Finding the Right Fit to Soar

Morgan Edwards

My journey started at the young age of 14, the summer right before high school, when I started working at my cousin's accounting firm. I continued working there throughout high school and into college. I learned a lot about accounting, money management, and how small businesses operated.

Little did I know; I took it for granted.

After graduating college, only a month before my 21st birthday, I immediately started working within corporate America. I stumbled through learning all of the rules, structures, and even office politics. Navigating the workplace was a lot more complex than it needed to be, especially at a job that had over 160,000 employees. It took me about four years to realize that it was not a place that I wanted my journey to end.

Yes – I made decent money.

No – I wasn't over worked.

I was at a job where I was left unhappy and unfulfilled and just going through the motions like a ghost.

I craved more. I didn't see my value in the workplace. I didn't see the impact that my day-to-day work was making in the larger scale of business. I didn't feel appreciated. Honestly, I took for granted the experiences I had faced at my first job. Not only did I miss the laid-back family atmosphere and flexible hours, but I desired to feel valuable, and craved a freedom that I once witnessed my dad and cousin had at the accounting firm where I spent a number of years working. I missed knowing that the work that I was doing mattered and impacted others.

At the age of 23 and determined to find that freedom I craved, I took a leap of faith and decided to start my entrepreneurial journey. I loved to travel and wanted that freedom-based lifestyle; so, I started by opening up my own travel agency. Well, why not? I dreamed of constantly traveling the world and what better way to do that than helping others travel as well? Well, that enjoyment only lasted about a year. Why? Because I still wasn't making that impact in people's lives that I truly desired.

While trying to understand where I fit into the world and trying to find myself through the fog of unclear paths before my eyes. I realized that because of my corporate hatred I had developed— I tried to run completely away from my passion, *technology*. As much as I tried to run, I was still "geeking-out" on new tools and was still giddy whenever I spoke about it. Also, people were still coming to me for technical advice.

My mission became clear.

Throughout my entrepreneurial journey, I connected with many other entrepreneurs. I quickly realized that so many entrepreneurs were running complete businesses all alone while claiming to be the CEO, when in reality, they were the Chief Executive Officer, Chief Operations Officer, Chief Technology Officer, and even the Chief Marketing Officer. They were doing ALL THE THINGS. They were stressed out. Stretched so thin, they forgot why they had started their business in the first place and that passion they once knew was gone.

And that's how *Your Chief Tech Officer* was born.

I realized that I could use my passion for technology and serve others. I could help these entrepreneurs with their business systems and all the technology aspects and remove the technology burden off their shoulder if I became their business partner and "their" Chief Technology Officer. This would be one less hat for them to wear. This would be one less stressor for them to have to handle.

Once I stepped into this role, the impact I created grew quickly because this was something about which I was passionate and called to do. I could immediately witness the impact and value for these women that I created, which was something I was missing in my corporate job. I was able to give my clients more time, freedom to make more money, and more power and independence. They constantly told me they didn't have to worry because I was handling the back-end support for them while they were on vacation. One had more time to sell services and grow her tribe through livestreams because she didn't have to focus on troubleshooting issues or managing systems and ultimately sold out her first course, making over thirty thousand dollars in sales in one week.

My clients are entrepreneurs who are growing and scaling their businesses. They desire to focus on serving their clients and spreading their mission. In order to impact their client's lives, they need to remain focused and stress-free. Technology and systems are their weak points and they have no desire to learn it. They want someone on their team-who understands their vision and can help to navigate them there. They are beyond tired of one-on-one services and are implementing new revenue streams through courses and sales funnels.

My clients receive a full 180-degree transformation. Most have gone through the hiring and firing process before for starting their business. They are at their wits-end trying to find someone that meshes well with them and delivers on the promises. When working with me, my clients know that the high-level support-they desire is there.

The impact I provide-with my services goes far beyond me. I help my clients spread their missions to the world. I now create my own value through my talents and passion instead of having a company define me and choose my income level based upon their perceived value.

There are always challenges on the entrepreneurial journey. First, the decision to become an entrepreneur is always a big one. I kept wondering to myself, *what would everyone think about my decision.* I felt as if they would judge me because wasn't my job paying me more than enough? Then, the fear and negative thoughts came rushing back as I transitioned from being a travel agent to technical support for online businesses. What will my audience say? How will my mom take it? Why do I keep starting new businesses? Will you pick something and stick to it already!

I quickly came to learn that it was all in my head. None of my family or close friends judged me. They were happy for me and supported me. It was me. I was afraid of stepping into my brilliance. I was afraid that people wouldn't think I knew what I was talking about, despite my extensive technological background, despite my experience. Once I made that conscious decision to say, "This is me. This is what I am doing" and make that incremental step forward, it immediately became worth it.

Throughout this journey, I've learned that if you don't believe in yourself and have the confidence that you indeed know what you're doing, no one else will. The confidence wasn't always in me; I had feelings of unworthiness or Imposter Syndrome. I had to remember that those thoughts were just in my head, remind myself that I am worthy. I am valuable. Someone will see my value and pay the price I set for my services. She is out there, and she is looking for me! She just hasn't found me yet.

The growth my business has achieved has been nothing short of amazing. In the next two years, *Your Chief Tech Officer*, will have a larger team and my company will be able to offer more holistic technology service. I will not only course launch support and funnel creation, but I will also be adding web design, SEO management, as well as online advertising services. I see *Your Chief Tech Officer* blooming and becoming an agency full of experts that can handle the varying needs that online businesses face.

I see *you;* ambitious entrepreneur. Don't give up. Just as I had to go through different experiences to find the right fit, you too will eventually find the right environment that stimulates you!

Your breakthrough is coming, Queen.

A Queen Boss is a woman who knows her abilities and steps completely into that light. She is passionate about what she does and doesn't let anyone make her feel 'less than'. She knows she is worthy and fully capable in supporting her mission.

I am a Queen Boss and I am valuable.

You are a Queen Boss and you are valuable.

Here's my business contact information:

Website: www.yourchieftechofficer.com

Email: hello@yourchieftechofficer.com

Facebook: www.facebook.com/yourchieftechofficer.com

Writing My Own Script: Courageously Creative

Srebrenica Lejla

Email: sb@thelivelycreative.com

Website: www.thelivelycreative.com

FB/IG: @srebrenicalejla

Chapter 10

Writing My Own Script: Courageously Creative

Srebrenica Lejla

No one wants to live a life unfulfilled. That's how I felt after graduating from college and getting a reasonably decent job in my desired field of pharmacy. I had done all the right things I was expected to do. Finish college; go into a career I romanticized when I was younger and even enjoyed once I started. However, this Millennial gal right here still did not feel fulfilled. I just knew there was something more I needed to be doing in my life. There was no way in hell I would only work, pay bills, (do a little travel here and there), and die. I'm sure many of us have heard this statement before.

Working in corporate America has its pros and cons for me, like anyone else. However, I was a recent graduate, a 20-something, wanting to live life on my terms. The first thing that struck a nerve with me was the asking and bidding to take time off from work. Whether it was for a doctor's appointment, weekend travel, or just a mental health care day, the idea of having to wait for my manager's approval to do things outside of my Monday-Friday, 9-5 made me feel stuck in the smallest box. Didn't my job know I had a life outside of this? How can they tell me what I can and cannot do with my time? It got to the point where I would get anxiety to request time off because of the uncertainty of the time not getting approved. As an I moved up the career ladder and to better positions, my pay increased but so did the stress. Although requesting time off was less stressful, I found myself being extraordinarily overworked and realistically, underpaid. I sat there and thought to myself, "Here I am going over and beyond for a job that can replace me at the drop of a dime." Even with the money and investments I had in place, there was still something missing in my life: freedom.

My journey began at this time. I needed to find what made Srebrenica happy. I needed to know the real me. I went back to what I knew best as a child: writing. Writing has been something which I've always enjoyed. I remember during talent shows, I would write dope poems on a whim and the crowd would be amazed at the words I had seamlessly put together just five minutes prior. Right before I finished college in 2016, I slowly got back into writing. You're supposed to know what you're doing with your life at the age of 18, at least that's what they make it seem. Creative writing has been an extreme catalyst for change for me. I've gotten closer with myself and achieved clarity on the many changes I was beginning to endure. I unleashed my creativity through writing.

I evolved as a young, Black Woman and found other creative things I enjoyed such as baking (like really, who knew?), crafty DIY projects for furniture, and my genuine love for art museums that heavily influences my writing. When I was able to enter all these things, that was the moment I felt free, like I had so much more purpose. It was like meeting a new version of me.

My goal is to ensure that individuals are confident and bold in expressing their creativity. In my book, *Be Free, Live Creatively*, I walk creatives from all phases to own their creative genius and learn how they too can create a positive impact. Our creativity nourishes purpose in life.

As a heart-centered entrepreneur, my frustration is seeing people feel like they are permanently committed to their current situations. I am showing people that it is okay to venture off into things they genuinely enjoy; even if that means disturbing the status quo. I want to see people, and especially, Black Women, live freely. We take on so many responsibilities, give advice, developed an entire culture the world craves and can't live without the influence. We deserve happiness and freedom to fulfill ourselves within. The impact I'm creating is to get people to think differently on their approach on life. As a Copywriting Strategist, I specifically help small business owners convey their story through magnetic messaging and thrive in their businesses. I started with assisting writers in general, adequately express themselves.

Everyone has a story to be told. Everyone has an impact to create. However, many people struggle with effectively articulating that message. I took advantage of this window to help businesses thrive. My clients are business owners who are in the first years of their entrepreneurial journey. I assess their brand and their story and create rewarding marketing messages that attract and convert their ideal clients. I make the process much more comfortable, so they are not spending endless hours figuring out the right words to say to their people. I am the witty word developer!

Never in a million years would I have thought I'd be taking my writing seriously as a profession. I soon realized it was much more than merely writing. I love seeing the transformation someone experiences when they look at the work they've created. Helping creative writers understand the power in their own messaging provides an excellent reward. Although I enjoy creating marketing messages for businesses, I much enjoy assisting other writers in perfecting their craft of writing and reel their audience in with an authentic voice and perspective.

Getting to that 'ah-ha' moment was not the easiest. I kept getting in my way. The biggest challenge for me was showing up. I knew I had the juice and skill to do what I do, but I was so reluctant because it required people to see me in a different light.

Through many episodes of trial and error, I noticed how beautifully I've grown. I now take my failures as required lessons learned, and I move to fail forward. Once I gained confidence, through the many lessons learned, things immediately changed for me. I began to achieve real, paying clients, but I encountered another challenge of consistency. For some reason, I had this unconscious thinking that once I got my clients, I could breathe and take a break. That is not the case. I now had the people I wanted and the people that needed me. I could not stop and let them down. It took me quite a bit to realize that I was entering into the actualization of my entrepreneurial journey. It's kind of like that moment when you finally get what you ask for then become perplexed when it manifests. The saying, "words don't hurt" is completely BS, coming from a Wordsmith like myself.

The moments I was afraid to step up and show up was due to my internal fear; fear that people would not believe in me; fears that this business I began was just a 'phase,' fear of complete failure. The truth is, people will think that, especially those whom you'd think would support you the most. It's imperative to understand and clarify your mission and purpose. Once that is solidified, you are unstoppable!

Next to the money. Money, Money, Money! I had to press through so many money blocks to achieve elevation and growth. Before, and even during the beginning stages of my entrepreneurial journey, I struggled with the connection between money and freedom. I had to change the way I viewed money. Mentally, I created barriers because of my fears. Most of the negative views I had about money as an adult came from the experiences I had with money as a child. I saw viewing having much money as a negative thing because the adults around me would preach that it's best to live a simple life. Alternatively, I'd overhear conversations about rich people and how ridiculous it was that they spent X amount of dollars on an item. I didn't want to have the reputation of someone who wasted money like those rich people. Over time, I had the mindset of 'less money, fewer problems.' That is such a terrible oxymoron, but it was the only way I was guided to think. When I first started working with Erica Stepteau, none of that made sense at the time. It took deep reflection for me to see my behavior and perspectives towards money. Although I am a person who delves in luxury things, I still had crazy abundance and money blocks.

Leaping into entrepreneurship is something that has been within me before I even accepted this new path. Everyday entrepreneurship is a choice, also when you find yourself well developed. You still must show up. For any women out there, who are hesitating to pivot themselves into a new level and delve into entrepreneurship, go for it! My hesitation, overthinking, and lack of confidence led me into almost four years of battling the vicious cycle of wanting to live in my purpose, but I always found myself talking out of it.

Nothing will be perfect, but everything will happen right on time if you allow.

I started my business off with the need to live freely with the actions of tapping into my creativity. Walking into my path as a writer has genuinely evolved. My goal is to help Creatives be more confident in their skill of writing and allow themselves on the road to create impact. In two years, I see my business evolving into a consulting firm. I look to work with business owners who need expertise in maintaining power in their messaging to connect with their clients.

I also look forward to teaching evolving writers the proper tools for effective copywriting.

To be a Queen Boss, you have to be sure of who you are and the purpose you have been chosen to fulfill. It is necessary to be unapologetic, authentically connect with soul clients, and achieve financial goals without fear.

Fashioned from Passion

Cindy May

Contact us Email- bossCqueens@gmail.com

Instagram- @bossCqueens

Website: www.bossCqueen.wordpress.com

Facebook- Facebook.com/bossCqueens

Chapter 11

Fashioned from Passion

Cindy May

A great life is doing what you want to do instead of doing what you have to do! Ask yourself, how would life be if money didn't exist? Would I have chosen my current profession, or would I have done what truly makes me happy? I chose the latter. Sometimes it takes a lifetime for people to come to this realization. Once the focus is your passion and no longer monetary gain, your life will change for the better. Therefore, it is important to follow your dreams because that is when you truly begin to live. Personally, it took a lot of persistence and courage to follow my dreams, but it is all finally paying off. I am a financial expert and an economically friendly personal stylist that teaches about financial freedom and resourcefulness, with years of experience as a corporate banker along with a personal styling business. I'm finally at a point in my life where I can say I have found true happiness by gifting the universe with my talents, and so can you!

As happy as the story is currently, it was not always so easy. Due to numerous factors, I waited until much later in life to cultivate my own passions. As a very young child, my family and I moved from a small-town city in Mississippi to Cleveland, Ohio. I was African American attending a predominantly Caucasian school. My memories there were happy. Our focus was on education and development. We were taught that monetary things had less value and that real value comes from knowledge. Back then, fashion was the least of my priorities and I never thought twice about it. As I got older, my family and I had to move, and I was forced to learn a different way of life.

I experienced culture shock during middle school years when I started attending a more diverse urban school. My initial belief was that material things did not matter; education was more important.

73

The only problem was, new peers didn't agree with that ideology. It was unpopular to wear shoes and clothes that weren't "in style." As a child, I witnessed myself and others get bullied for lack of material things. Fortunately, the lessons learned during that timeframe positively affected my future. In hindsight, having the opportunity to be placed in multiple environments gave me the ability to see various perspectives that helped along my journey.

In human nature we are highly likely to assimilate to our environments. Therefore, I began to tap into my creative side. My family was middle class, with limited funds; however, I would do chores, save money, and hack my clothes in an innovative way just to look nice. Because of my efforts, compliments from others became a daily occurrence, resulting in confidence in my abilities. During my free time, sketching prom dresses in my notebook was my favorite hobby. One day, during high school, I told a family member about my dreams of becoming a fashion stylist and I didn't get the response I longed for. I was told that I shouldn't go to college for fashion because there is simply no demand for fashion in Cleveland, Ohio. Instead, I should go to college for a career in the medical field. Momentarily, my dreams were crushed.

I had officially been placed in a box that I had to fight to get out of. Graduating high school was easy, but picking a major was so difficult. Subconsciously, my mind started replaying the conversation I had with my family member again. I started telling myself, "I would never be financially secure as a stylist." As a result, I went to college and majored in psychology. I was interested in psychology; however, it was never my passion. I remember on school days I would have to drag myself out of bed regularly. After all of my internal battles I finally came to the conclusion that this is not how I want my life to be. Therefore, I took a break from college and dived directly into the work field. One of the hardest decisions in life is whether to follow your dreams or to pursue the dreams that others have for you, so I urge you to choose wisely!

Life has a funny way of aligning us with our sole purpose. After much persistence, I had finally landed my first corporate job interview. On the surface, there were feelings of excitement; underneath, my nerves were through the roof! Starting a new career has a unique way of humbling us. Although I had most resources needed to obtain the job, I lacked one thing: proper attire. For the first time in years, I had felt intimidated about my appearance. I had recently gained a large amount of weight and my clothes no longer fit. Not to mention, I was also stepping into a career with powerhouses and I was unsure if I would fit in. I was very overwhelmed and worried. Luckily, that feeling did not last long. Upon searching within myself and identifying the emotions, I began to embrace them.

Developing the understanding that anything that is tangible is not valuable was a very profound moment! I realized that it is not about how much the clothes cost, it is about how you feel about yourself first. I started doing spiritual practices like meditating, saying affirmations, and journaling to find myself. If you ever happen to feel lost along your journey, doing these activities can help you tremendously! It feels like seeing life through different lenses. It equipped me with a new sense of confidence in myself and my gift. I became so inspired that I would crop pictures of models and celebrities and recreate their look for more than half the price. I would wear those outfits and get so many compliments. It was at that moment that I knew I was on my way to becoming a Queen Boss.

My career and business were officially in perfect alignment. I had obtained a corporate career at a financial institution in a department that helped businesses track spending and create budgets. I also created a business of my own, which focused on women saving time and money on fashion. Incorporating the knowledge obtained from my career was also applied to my business. I learned great customer services skills and financial literacy. It is a blessing to have multiple sources of income during your financial journey because it can be very difficult to operate with lack of funds. My career and life experiences taught me how to be responsible with capital. It taught me the importance of credit and tracking spending. So not only am I a great personal stylist, I am also an expert on financial management. My goal is to merge fashion and finance together in perfect harmony. I want Queens to look like a million bucks while simultaneously maintaining their financial well-being.

My two-year vision for my business is to help women create the lifestyle they desire. I want to be a fence for women to get to the next level professionally and financially. My soul client is a woman who is elevating, whether it is physically, professionally, or spiritually. I have a signature program that I am confident will help Queens with elevation. It includes assessing the client's body size and giving them tips on what to wear to highlight their best features. I also offer an assessment to get an understanding of their likes and dislikes in regard to attire so that I can easily present them with a beautiful look that they will love. The best part of the program is the financial wellness portion that helps them track their spending, to free up capital to allocate to other places. Most importantly, I assist with mindset coaching because the mind is the most powerful aspect in evolution. The reason I am so passionate about helping women is that I have been in their shoes. I have had to transition so many times in life from moving to new locations to changing careers and even weight fluctuation. It can be very difficult on the path to evolution. Therefore, I am very confident in my ability to push women to the next level.

My ultimate goal was to collaborate with other like-minded consultants and build a team. My team consists of the following: fashion, finance, business and mindset coaches. We formulated a team with the sole purpose of helping our clients elevate their perspective from the inside out. We start with the mindset coaching, teaching them how to build their confidence. Then, we help them upgrade their wardrobe to help them look as amazing as they feel. Lastly, the business and finance coaching portion, will help them save money to allocate additional funds towards their future endeavors. Our goal is for not only our team to win, but for every Queen we take under our wing to have a victory as well. We will all rise to become Queen Bosses!

Contact us Email- bossCqueens@gmail.com

Instagram- @bossCqueens

Website- www.bossCqueen.wordpress.com

Facebook- Facebook.com/bossCqueens

The Queen Boss Rise

The Making of a Millennial Marketer

Brittney Moffatt

Website: accordingtobrittney.com.

Instagram: @accordingtobrittney

🌿 Chapter 12

The Making of a Millennial Marketer

Brittney Moffatt

During my senior year of high school, I was the student who would run into the counselor's office every day to see what new college information they had. In a short time, I had accumulated a collection of college magazines, flyers, and all the information one could have about college. I was ready. I had big dreams and I knew that they would begin in this next chapter of my life - starting in college. I was going to rule undergrad, graduate and then, rule the "real world." A great job, great money, and a happy life were all heading my way.

I had a great upbringing, despite my mom being a single mother raising two daughters on virtually one income. I never felt like I didn't have enough. Some would even say I was spoiled as I got a lot of experiences that my friends didn't. My mom took us on vacations, we always shopped for new clothes each school year, and the Christmas tree were always full of presents.

As I grew up, I started to see and understand our situation. It was far from easy for my mother to be able to provide for us. She worked at a job she didn't like that grossly underpaid her. She would come home tired, annoyed and looking for other income avenues like running her own business.

I knew that I didn't want that for myself. The job I had was going to be something I enjoyed, and I wanted to be grossly overpaid.

The Start of My Self-Discovery

As I'm applying for colleges, I am thinking all about what field I want to go into. This was the first time I really did some soul searching. The field I choose would have to offer jobs that were fulfilling yet prosperous.

I started with things I like to do because "Do what you love," right? As I started looking back on my childhood, I thought about the times I created gifts. For my mother's birthday one year, I wrote a magazine all about her and her day. She kept that crudely drawn and eagerly written magazine on her dresser for years.

When my family came to visit from Georgia, I hand wrote each of them a newspaper announcing their arrival and what to expect during their visit. I remember that they laughed when I gave them each an individual paper. Families normally share one newspaper, but I wrote one for everyone.

My grandmother gave me a gift that I will never forget - blank books by *American Girl*. These books were meant to be used to tell your own story. I was gifted two books and filled them both with fictional characters and plots. Looking back, it was clear where my passion lay. I was destined to be a writer.

Now that I knew that writing was my path, it was time to select a major. Of course, I chose journalism. What better way to write than to be a journalist? Okay, got the college spirit, got the major, and after plenty of applications, I got into college. You would think that I would be ecstatic, which I was, but there was still something missing in my career journey.

A Solid Direction

As soon as I got to college, I joined the school newspaper. This is when I learned something else about myself. I'm an introvert who is terrified of talking to people. My first assignment for the newspaper was to interview someone for my article. How was I going to do this? Writing is my jam, but talking? To people? No, thank you. I completed the assignment, but it was the first and last article I did for the school paper. This experience made me start questioning my decision to be a journalist. So, it was time to go back to the drawing board.

What else did I love besides writing? Business. I knew I wanted to be successful and fulfilled. That could definitely come from running my own business. My mom had a side hustle for as long as I can remember. Her first hustle I remember was selling light up novelties at festivals when I was in high school. She loved that business and used it to honor her mother by calling it Cocoa's Delights (Geraldine "Cocoa" Smith). Now, she sells Paparazzi jewelry which she also loves on top of her job. Being an entrepreneur was something that really stood out to me, probably from looking up to my mother.

How can I mix my love of writing with my love of business? My first thought was to build from the ground up and run my own magazine geared towards helping women be more body positive. So, many people close to me have struggled with their weight and I felt called to speak on it. The next step was changing my major to business.

Changing my major proved to be difficult because my GPA was not high enough to get accepted into the business school at my college. Well, that was a setback. Now, I had to figure out Plan B. I talked to my counselor who listened to my idea of owning a business. I recall being a bit embarrassed to talk about my dreams. She recommended studying communications with a minor in entrepreneurship. I was beyond excited because it was a perfect mix of both writing and business.

In my normal fashion, I decided to do "all the things." I got involved in the Association for Women in Communications on campus. Literally, nominated myself to be President, even though I wasn't a part of the organization prior. Next was the Entrepreneurship club, and yes, I went for President there, too. I didn't get it, but I did get to be the social media chair. How's that for coincidence?

We got our first computer when I was about 10 years old, so, the internet has been a part of my life for a while. It started with games and kids' stuff and evolved into social networking as a teen. Although, I probably shouldn't have, I had a ton of social media profiles online (don't worry, they are all deleted). I was so intrigued at being able to connect with people through that box on my desk.

Everything finally felt in place. I was in the right major, right students' groups, and even had a business idea.

Until I started to lose passion for that idea. Starting a magazine just wasn't shaping out to be my path, but social media was. While looking at what's out there and accessing what I wanted to do, the words 'marketing' and 'social media' were standing out to me.

Discovering My Career

I knew I was finally onto something. The combination of writing and business was marketing. I could pursue both my passions and be prosperous. This was my moment to pursue something I would enjoy. To me, that was more important than anything, to love what I was doing.

Fast forward to now, I look back on all those experiences and how they shaped the entrepreneur I am today. The failures, the self-discovery, the characteristics of a child that would one day turn into a tenacious Queen who is certain about her dreams. I truly believe and have always believed that I am destined for greatness.

My passion, dedication, and ambition have led me here. This content writer and social media strategist was once a young girl who liked to write for fun or create social media profiles. I was the girl who thought my words were a gift that I share with my family. Now, writing is gift I give to my clients as a professional writer - and myself as an entrepreneur.

My writing helps other people grow their businesses which for a girl with a passion for business and writing, I'd say this is a pretty cool journey.

You can learn more about me and my services at accordingtobrittney.com. You can also follow me on Instagram @accordingtobrittney.

The Queen Boss Rise

Mirror, Mirror

Aisha Quinn

Email: QueenBoss79@outlook.com

Facebook: Aisha Quinn

Instagram: aisha.quinn1

Chapter 13

Mirror, Mirror

Aisha Quinn

"No eyes have seen, no ears have heard, and no mind has imagined what God has prepared for those who love Him."

--1 Corinthians 2:9

My Why

I hated the reflection I saw when I looked boldly into the mirror. Staring back at me stood a woman with a "dream deferred." With five mouths to feed, and no husband to help shoulder the mountain of responsibility, I felt stupid and ignorant. How could I be so dumb to be in this situation...again? But I fell for it.

"No need for protection," he whispered. "I'll be here for you no matter what happens."

His touch hypnotized me, giving me temporary amnesia to his previous baby mama drama. I knew he meant nothing he said, but the man had the SWAGG, that left me speechless (let your mind fill in the blank). Unfortunately, he wasn't shooting any, and I ended up pregnant with number six.

Depression ate away the final morsels of my self-esteem, pulling me down with each self-destructive thought. I attempted to find my worth in people who were also broken, pouring myself into their lives in hopes that they would heal me. They couldn't. Only God had the capacity to do that. Despite all my attempts at finding love and hoping someone would finally love me, I came to the hard conclusion that I had to learn to love myself first.

For six months, I numbed my feelings. I honestly felt like a zombie hiding behind makeup and smiles, putting on my game face for all to see. I didn't know how to love myself. I needed a man to do that. Why wasn't God sending him? In my anger and frustration, I called out to God!

No, let me be honest, I yelled at God with rage and disappointment. I cried one of those ugly cries, having what I thought was a justified tantrum. After a while, I grew tired of my own self and just stopped. I lay there on my tear-soaked pillow, heavily breathing through my mouth unable to breathe through my stuffy nose. It was in that moment, it was like God said, "Finally, I can talk to you now." Like a soft kiss upon my cheek, he whispered to my heart ever so gently.

"I've always loved you, and I have always been there." God reminded me of my worth and the "WHY" of my existence was born.

My Impact:

Thousands of women suffer from childhood traumas and experiences that alter their self-esteem, leaving them open like books so easily read by students of "the game" ...the varsity "players" waiting to prey on their wounded hearts. So many looking for the fathers they never had, hoping to provide that father for their child. Like a reflection in the mirror, the cycle of single parenthood continues, leaving another little girl, disguised as a grown woman, crying out in silence as she unknowingly gives her most prized possession away (her body). Hoping to gain the world of her dreams, she gives of herself one more time, only to relive that same familiar nightmare when he no longer returns her calls.

The roller coaster of disappointment, abandonment, emotional, and physical abuse can take a woman a lifetime to find the courage to stop the ride and get off. Some will never pull the lever because they have grown accustomed to the drama the ride provides. They would feel out of place in a healthy environment, subconsciously creating ways to venture back on the ride while blaming someone else for the chaos.

I know what it's like. Because of first-hand knowledge, I will never judge another woman for the actions she commits in her broken state of mind. At times, I felt like my life was being played out on a stage with 10,000 people watching me fight for true love, withholding nothing.

When these performances failed, people expected me to get over the hurt. Well, it's not so easy to move on, especially when you have children in tow that look just like him.

Despite the heartache, there is hope. The Bible says, "Joy comes in the morning." Your test can become your testimony and your morning is whenever you choose to rise up and acknowledge the truth that you control your response to the way the world treats you. So, take the time you need to mourn. Don't let anyone rush you through that process. When you are ready, you will know. As long as you have breath in your body, you have another chance to set things straight--to experience the joy of the Lord. You will soon discover it is your time to shin, your time to decide to win.

All of the things that I've endured throughout my life--things imposed upon me and things I have imposed upon myself, can be used as character builders. I want to impact the lives of women through the stories of my life. My hope is that by being vulnerable, I can help to open doors for women around the world to share their stories as they journey to self-love and healing. Our passion and dreams are worth the work. As a close friend would say, "Put on your big girl panties and let's get it!"

My Client

My clients are black women who simply have given up on life. They are women between the ages of 22-55 years young -- women who think they can't make it. My goal is to help them see that it is okay to be your authentic you and still be loved in the right way. We are Queens and NOT bitches, hoes, and sluts. I want them to know that we don't have to take our clothes off to be a woman of greatness -- a Queen.

As a Queen, you can change your mindset to achieve your dreams and goals. Having a mindset change is very important in the process of changing your life. I have created, *The Mirror-Mirror Movement - Five Ways a Woman can Change her Mindset in 90 Days*.

This program helps women step up and live out their truth and inspires them to be successful. The following are the six steps they will take on this journey to becoming the Queen they were destined to be:

Step One: Starts by writing the vision and making it plain.

Step Two: Examine who they are... bad, good, or indifferent, and make steps toward future plans.

Step Three: Set goals for changing their mindset as Queens

Step Four: Identify their past hurts and overcome them

Step Five: Affirm and self-motivate to go after their dreams and finish what they start.

Contact info: QueenBoss79@outlook.com

https://www.instagram.com/aisha.quinn1

The Queen Boss Rise

Leaning into the Shifts

Dr. Jackie E. Phillips

Email: jackie@drjackiephillips.com

Website: Drjackiephillips.com

Chapter 14

Leaning into the Shifts

Dr. Jackie E. Phillips

God, indeed, has a vision for your life. You may not see it all at once, but I am here to remind you to trust the process. When God is ready to take you to a higher calling in your life, He creates a radical shift, which switches life as usual into a crisis.

Over the past five years of my life, I have gone through several major shifts which has directed my path into my purpose and elevated my business. These shifts may require a period of isolation, obedience, and discernment as you lean into God's voice in the midst of your crisis. Mastering each stage of the shift prepares you for your elevation. As I look back, I can now see how God can create certain **Shifts** in your life to **Transform** you into the person you are today. This transformation not only represents me as a person, but the developmental stages and growth of my business thus far.

My first major shift in my life began in July 2014. During this period, my world came tumbling down. On the heels of divorce after 17 years of marriage, I then became unemployed. Totally stripped from the security of a marriage and a full-time job, I received the directive to start my own business, Life Changer's Writers and Healing Institute. This was a season of total surrender, obedience, and a faith walk., a season where I put my faith into action and confirmed the statement that *the Lord will take care of all my needs.*

I had a three-year grace period to start my company before I totally lost my employment. Within that time-period, I bargained with God, worrying that my business would not be able to sustain me. I believed that I needed to find another full-time job. I became very persistent in that direction, while at the same time, moved forward in growing the business.

My last day of full-time employment, June 30, 2017, was the hallmark of the next major shift in my life. It not only marked my last day of full-time employment, but the end of a season. The very next day, I stepped into my business full-time, since none of my efforts towards a full-time job had materialized. It was indeed a time of mixed and ambivalent feelings. It was fear of the unknown, yet trust that my God "got my back." The words of God keep ringing in my spirit, "Do you trust me?" This was a season of reliving the words of the 23rd Psalm, "The Lord is My Shepherd," and how God provided for me during that troublesome season of my life. The first six months were the most challenging, but were comprised of both high and low experiences, which sometimes came at the same time. Financially, I was struggling, getting behind on my bills, and increasing my debt. However, I also got many opportunities to expand my business and **Soar into Greatness**.

Being sandwiched between both experiences didn't allow me to stay in the valley for too long. I was able to see my breakthrough and capitalized on the resources and support from my village. A sense of joy stabilized me and prevented me from sinking deep down into the valley. In addition, I was able to invest in two wonderful coaches who have guided me toward growing and developing my business. Today, I am on the other side of that crisis. Yes, I may feel that I may not be where I want to be financially, but God reminds me to continue trusting Him and I am confident He always feeds his sheep.

The third major shift brought a sense of clarification of my purpose and gifting in life. My mission as a **Mid-Wife of Purpose** and a **Spiritual Healer** is to ignite the spirit of individuals so that they can **Soar into Greatness**. In doing so, I awaken individuals to the healing and transformative sides of their life's story. The pain and turmoil associated with our valley experiences can sometimes create a depressive state in people. Without the right support and resources, many people may remain stuck in their valley experiences for several years. Getting to the other side of the journey is indeed a transformation and one through which I can usher individuals

Therefore, through my company, Life Changers' Writing and Healing Institute, I empower individuals to write, heal, and create impact by sharing their stories. This transformative process enables my clients, or **Life Changers,** to ignite their warrior spirits to create impact within their communities as they document and share their life stories into chapters in anthologies or publishing their own personal books.

I have worked with over 100 individuals, helping them in healing, writing, publishing and sharing their stories. Over the past three years, we have produced three anthologies with an average of 15 to 20 authors who all write a chapter sharing their stories. This year, we are in the process or releasing two anthologies: *Prayer Works* and *Triumph, Our Cancer Story.* Many of these individuals have then moved to the next step of producing their individual books through our company as well. For the first half of 2019, we have produced 10 authors, with many more in the pipeline.

As a Mid-Wife of Purpose and bestselling author, I also awaken individuals to their **Call to Greatness** through my books, seminars, and motivational speeches. I have published two of my own personal books, *The Greatness Within You* and *The Purpose Factor.* In addition, I have participated in three compilations: *Stand up to be Heard* and *Women Across Borders.*

The fourth major shift happened in 2019, with the development of the book project, *The Power of the Valley.* In compiling and conducting research for this book, I developed the **Power of the Valley Framework**. This framework is grounded on the process of transformation as one goes through valley periods in life. **The Power of the Valley Framework** illustrates the five stages of transformation one passes through from moment of impact by a crisis to the ascent of soaring to the next mountain top.

The five stages of this Framework are as follows: Impact, Emotional Paralysis, Break Through, Wholeness and Harvest. Each stage happens both in your conscious and your subconscious. The conscious level illustrates the actions you take as you endure the turmoil associated with the crisis, while the subconscious transformation demonstrates the development of a seed of greatness which carries the tools needed for your next mountain-top assignment. The development of **The Seed of Greatness** is measured by your mindset and actions taken in the conscious level.

The subconscious transformation gives birth to the **Seed of Greatness** that will enable you to soar to your next mountain-top experience. Therefore, it is very important for that seed to develop, grow, and germinate. The length and time in each phase will vary from person to person. Progressing through each stage takes place on a continuum with the goal of moving through the five stages. How you move through each stage determines your actions of being stagnant, sporadic, or consistent and intentional. These actions are measured on a Progression Scale from 0 – 5; with level 0 being no activity and level 5 demonstrating intentional and consistent actions within that stage. Being stagnant for lengthy periods indicates the need for external support and resources. You may have maxed out the use of your own abilities to push through the situation.

For my authors in the Institute, taking this bold step in writing and sharing their stories is not an easy process, but with determination they persisted. During their writings, they all revisited their trauma and their pain, pushing past the shame and guilt that may have been associated with their stories. Through this nine-month process, they deconstruct their journey in defining the meaning and purpose to each participant's narrative. Their journey is marked by the following steps as they processed and wrote their depictions of how they each came to understand the meaning of the Power of their valleys:

1. Identify the point of impact and events that led up to the crisis.

2. Evaluate their state of mind while they experienced emotional paralysis.

3. Recognize when they reached a breakthrough of hope during their valley experience.

4. List what strategies and support they used to diminish the symptoms of the crisis.

5. Analyze where they are on the journey towards **Wholeness.** Have they moved into a stage of healing, restoration, and renewal?

6. What are the energy blocks or dead areas that are showing up in their lives?

7. Discover what a season of harvest means to their story. How can they enhance or develop a platform to create impact and share their story and talents in the marketplace?

As I write this chapter, I am in the process of this final, major shift, the launching of the I Am My Story Campaign. This campaign is driven by my determination to create an empowerment movement of Life Changers who are ready to be awakened to their Call to Greatness. Through this campaign, my mission is to go on a national book and media tour where we will empower over 100 individuals to heal, write, and share their stories over the next year. My mission is not only for my authors, but to empower as many people as possible.

There is power and healing by sharing our stories. Going through a valley period is not an easy journey. Such an occurrence requires us to lean into the shifts that occur in our lives. To lean in requires, persistence, determination, faith, endurance, and support. In pushing through, we can get to the other side as renewed and transformed persons. Such a transformation brings a restored mindset that reveals the need to lean toward a life of greatness and service. Furthermore, surviving a major, life crisis prepares you for other crises which will indeed show up in your life. The blessing you receive is that your resiliency and rate of recovery will be much faster in moving through your valley.

My journey has become my story, one of leaning into my shifts, thus becoming transformed, healed, and moving into a stage of wholeness. Being obedient to God's will and trusting in the process will help bring us to the **Other Side**.

How has your journey transformed your life's story? How have you leaned into the shifts in your life? The account is yours to tell and will bless the lives of others. Have you found meaning from your valley experiences? Or are you having difficulty navigating through your valley? To help you process and answer these questions, my mission is to provide a roadmap for you to understand the concept of the valley and the stages of transformation that occur during this process. Likewise, if you have a story to tell or you are ready to write your book, connect with me today.

Today, I would like to empower you to Share your Story and be a part of the I am My Story campaign. Connect with me if you have any questions or would like to be part of the Life Changers Healing and Writing Institue.

Email: jackie@drjackiephillips.com.

Website: Drjackiephillips.com

The Queen Boss Rise

Overweight, Overwhelmed, Over-Fifty to Fit, Faith-Filled and Financially Free

Dr. Karen Maxfield-Lunkin

Website: https://www.bridgeucation.com

Facebook: Dr. Karen Maxfield-Lunkin

Contact Info: bridgeucation88@gmail.com

﹝ Chapter 15

Overweight, Overwhelmed, Over-Fifty to Fit, Faith-Filled and Financially Free

Dr. Karen Maxfield-Lunkin

And we know that all things work together for good to them that love God, to them who are the called according to his purpose.

~Romans 8:28

My Very Specific Target Audience

I am speaking to that Woman of God over 50 who knows down in her soul that her purpose is NOT fulfilled, that she has much more to do.

I am speaking to the beautiful black woman over 50 who, like me – struggled through an era to fit in, assimilate, and separate from our blackness.

I am speaking to that woman over 50 who has awakened to find that you have not used your voice, you have not lived your life, you lost sight of God, you lost sight of who you are and Whose you are.

The woman over 50 who is overweight and overwhelmed with life. You looked at yourself in the mirror and shocked that you had let yourself go.

You are a believer in Christ, but you have not allowed the power of God to work in your life either because you have been in control – trying hard not to get hurt again.

I am talking to the woman over 50 who still has dreams and aspirations, but you feel like you may have waited too late, that you've made too many mistakes.

They may feel that they have messed up financially, relationally, or literally may have missed their God calling because of fear or religious tradition.

I am talking to the woman over 50 who feels like you have been asleep for the last 20 years and you are just now waking up.

I am speaking to you beautiful queen because you have spent your past few years grieving over past abuses, hurt, rape, that abortion you had as a teen, divorce, suicide attempts, career failures, ill-conceived relationships, bad blood between you and your own children, husband, parents, cousins and friends.

But most specifically – I sounding the clarion call for Kingdom Sistah Ambassadors over 50 in the African Diaspora, who is a born-again believer, detached from her roots, yearning to reconnect and go back to Africa literally and figuratively to stand on the soil and make peace with your past.

The Birth of an Idea

Overweight, Overwhelmed, Over-50 was conceived one day as I gazed in the mirror. I was disgusted with what I saw, completely frustrated with the amount of weight I had gained over the years - My financial situation was dire and overwhelming. My personal struggles compounded. My relationship with my husband of over 25 years at that time was less than functional at best. I was just here, existing. I was a wife. I was a mother of three adult children – one with special needs. I was a minister, a daughter of an aging parent, an entrepreneur, and a business owner – yet, I was a woman ready to explode.

What Compelled Me?

I believe that God's people, Kingdom citizens are meant to live abundantly – that we are supposed to enjoy wealth and not be tied down by debt, provision and poverty while here on this earth. I am compelled to tell *my* story – to not be ashamed of *my* roots, to embrace *my* beauty, body, skin, lips, hips, hair, swag, humor and matriarchal, queenly nature that God gave black women. I found God when I stopped chemically processing my hair, accepted the texture curl – I know that may make some uncomfortable, but those that understand will understand. My why is to show my beautiful girls who I introduced to this culture of self-hatred, their true Queenship.

We Should be Impacting the World, Not Shrinking from It.

Women of Color over 50 are walking out and breathing, stepping into their greatness and God given glory. I am impacting a generation of women who worked hard to be something other than who we are, suffocated, oppressed suffered under an identity crisis. We have suffered from a syndrome of throwing our own babies (visions and dreams) overboard to breastfeed someone else's vision, dream and purpose. I am impacting a nation, a generation, an era, a people – through these women.

The Creation of BridgeUcation Creative Education Consultants and Write2Heal Brand.

I originally created my business to meet that need of connecting passion to entrepreneurial endeavors. It started with a vision and dream first listed on a vision board. I wrote that I would host retreats, workshops; write and publish books and Literary coaching.

I have had to work on my own personal mindset first. I created a special prayer room / office in my 4th bedroom. I spent many hours listening to sermons and inspiring videos on mindset. It became clear that I had a great deal of healing work to do. I wrote in my journals, keeping tabs on my mindset. My family began to note the changes in me.

I Hired a Coach

With my coach, I was able to press through areas that in times past, I would have run the other direction. I was open and honest with my coach and told her that I needed her to hold me accountable. She did! With her help, I launched out into the deep and had my first ever Women Writing2Heal Year End Retreat – it was phenomenal. From there, I was able to hire my first clients – and they were high end clients! I closed on two clients within a day of my retreat. I was no longer questioning my own worth and skills. That mindset work and subsequent shift literally changed my life. I continue to work and unpeel the onion, but that was the catalyst.

OVERWEIGHT

I had to face that I had an eating disorder. I had to call it for what it was. I was addicted to fast food and I would use food as comfort instead of dealing with my emotions.

I want to tell you that God has a plan for you, for your body that He designed when He created us. YOU must take control of your eating. You must decide to work with God and your body to allow it to rest and heal.

I want you to know that YOU must take control of the food you put in your mouth, understand its nutritional value and if it is compatible to your genetic makeup. It's in my genes, the women in my family are prone to weight gain – but I was also living a sedentary life and not addressing my stress

Face the Trauma

I received the not-so-unexpected words from my health care practitioner that she wanted me to return for another glucose test to determine if I was pre-diabetic. *That did it!* As far as I was concerned, being pre-diabetic was like being a little bit pregnant. My Dad had been diagnosed as diabetic about ten years prior and I had the tell-tale signs of the huge belly, thirst and sugar cravings. The body is the temple of God. Take care of it. Changing my lifestyle was no longer an option.

Overwhelmed as I Faced the Trauma of my African Roots

I used poetry to face deep, ancestral trauma.
Some of us IGNORE who we are,
Some of us HATE who we are
Some of us HONOR others above us.
But all of us must MAKE PEACE with who we are.

Ancestral Rage: Science has revealed that ancestral memory can be passed down through DNA. That would lend itself to the notion that much of the many African Americans have lived in shame, drowned in anger and some acknowledged a disconnection that leaves us feeling lost, and disoriented. Marcus Garvey said, "A people without the knowledge of their past history, origin and culture is like a tree without roots." This healing I have experienced at the cellular level proved to be clues to my purpose.

Finding my Purpose: I recognize that I had to address the disconnect at the cellular level – just as Jesus admonished the Disciples that some things would not be addressed unless they prayed and fasted. I also knew that God's word spoke of visiting the sins from previous generations and how those things are passed down through the DNA. I realized that I had found my purpose! I must connect the natural and spiritual benefits of the biblical fasting the Jesus encouraged. I determined to study the scientific benefits of fasting to that would cause a healing from an ancestral transference. I knew that I had to share this learning with the Overweight, Overwhelmed, and Over-Fifty, embracing Romans 8:28

The African Roots Project Retreat was Born

In 2015 an idea was downloaded to me – Write2Heal: The African Roots Project Retreat. This would be the second book in the series, Write2Heal, so imagine my surprise and delight when I learned in December 2018, that the president of Ghana, announced that 2019 was the Year of Return for all people in the African Diaspora to return. As 2019 marked exactly 400 years since the first ship full of enslaved Africans landed in Jamestown, VA.

Upon returning to Ghana, West Africa in December of 2019, each co-author and myself will participate in several healing activities on the Motherland designed to reconnect us with our roots.

However, the greatest opportunity is to RETURN to REPENT for our ancestors and – to lift THE NAME of Jesus Christ, proclaiming Romans 8:28 to be true – truly, all things do work together for our good.

OVER-FIFTY

Physical Cleansing

At my age, I had to find out what was best for my body. I began a 21-day cleanse in March of 2017 at which time, I cut dairy, caffeine, sugar, gluten – yes, I did all at one time – for over two months.

After this process, I not only lost weight, but I was cured of that foggy thinking, my headaches were gone, and I had an overall sense of well-being. I had over-charged my liver for many years, and now it was able to dispel years of toxins – and it was working over-time. I increased my water intake, exercised, and sat in a dry sauna to help the process. I also took natural supplements, such as milk thistle and other bitter herbs, to further assist my liver in the process.

Spiritual Cleansing

Spiritually, I increased my prayer time, I read the Word of God more consistently. Most importantly, my relationship improved with my husband during this time, and I had an outlet to talk out what I was experiencing. During the next year, I began a series of fasting. I began the year with an extended water only fast, losing much weight, curing the pre-diabetes, bladder issues, rising blood pressure, eyesight improved, mental clarity returned and so much more.

During this time, I wrote in my journal to record my thoughts and the return of flowing creativity that I had missed for so long. Just like my body, my creativity was stifled because it was trapped inside of a toxic environment. I was amazed at how I could hear and see God at every turn and how quickly He was responding and answering my prayers.

My Advice - There's Power in the Pen

I sought to find the healing in my writing once again and I began to write to record the changes I was seeing in every area. I have even noted increased memory function, including word recall when in conversation. Writing – rather than eating – can clear the way for the healing that is needed.

Writing is one way to keep track of what you are eating and the effects of that food on your body the days after you've eaten it. In my case, eating is, and has been, a comforting addiction…yes, I call it an addiction – what else would you call placing something in your body that gives you immediate, very short-lived, satisfaction, but will certainly wreak havoc on that same body in the next few hours?

Writing empowered me to see the correlation between my health, my African roots and my compassion to write, heal and share.

I have learned a great deal in the process of writing and below I share four ways that writing promotes healing in the author.

1. **Writing allows us to make visible the thoughts and feelings we are having.**
2. **When talking isn't an option and prayer seems too hard, writing gives voice to our spirit and a release to allow us to stop and make sense of things**.
3. **Writing has been proven to improve our emotional and even physical well-being!** Writing presents a space for the writer to place negative emotions and puts a handle on them.
4. **Writing serves as a recorder for our lives giving us a historical marker to which we can refer, giving a rooted perspective.**
   Sometimes, the answer is in the historical records we have kept with our writing. We can review, revisit, rewrite, rework and quite possibly move beyond the current rut.
5. **Writing Changes our perspective.**
   We have the power, the poetic justice to reframe the story – perhaps with a fictional ending or allowing our character to confront an abuser. Even re-write the history of an oppressed African people!

I am committed to leave Overweight, Overwhelmed, Over-50 behind and step into Fit, Faith-filled and Financially Free life.

Call to Action and Conclusion

"When you see yourself as the Queen that you are, you shine, and those high vibrations attract success like a magnet." ~Erica Stepteau

Your Rise...

Remember Baylor Barbee's chess approach to life and business that changed my life and woke me up? Here it is again for you:

*"Every day you define your role: how you move, how you operate, how you plan. In chess, a pawn can move one space, at most two spaces. A Queen, on the other hand, can move in **ANY Direction**, as far as she wants. Think about your life. There are no limitations on how much you can accomplish in a day. No one will ever tell you that you've gone too far today, you've accomplished too much, and you must stop here. We place those limitations on ourselves sometimes. We don't strive for royalty; we settle for being pawns.*

God doesn't want that for us. God wants us to move about freely. He wants us to cover "the entire board." That's why He put us on it. In chess, inexperienced players usually sacrifice their pawns early in the game and try to protect "the important pieces. "Losing a pawn doesn't affect us., but losing a Bishop, a Queen, and especially a King, hurts us. In life, we define our roles based upon the decisions we make. Too many people lead careless, uncalculated lives, running right into devastation.

*Look at people you admire and look up to. There's a good chance that they live their lives as royalty. They put a solid support group around them. They work well with others. They make calculated moves and they plan very well. Aside from that, when it is time to make a move in life, they strike hard and cover a lot of ground. You can do the same. You **can** be a Queen Boss rising on the chess board of life. All it takes is a change in your mindset. You must live your life as a piece that matters, and subsequently, people around your will start treating you as such."*

Just as I radically overhauled my life and became devoted to helping and inspiring other women to do the same after reading this, each of the authors in this compilation used life's chess board to also "make moves" in their lives to be the **Queen Bosses** rising. Let our stories inspire you to embrace your own journey back to your throne.

So now, after reading the chapters, where are you on your journey towards becoming a Queen Boss? Which of the stories in this compilation inspired you? How can I assist you to reach your fullest potential?

1. **What's your "WHY?" What is your motivating factor for your walk towards your entrepreneurial journey?**

_____

_____

_____

_____

_____

_____

_____

_____

_____

2. WHAT Impact are you creating?

_____

_____

_____

_____

_____

_____

_____

_____

_____

_____

_____

_____

_____

3. Who are you called to serve?

_____

_____

_____

_____

_____

_____

_____

_____

_____

_____

_____

_____

_____

4. What transformation will your clients receive?

_____

_____

_____

_____

_____

_____

_____

_____

_____

_____

_____

_____

_____

5. **Describe your entrepreneurial journey thus far in relation to the following:**

   o **Challenges/ Rewards**

_____

_____

_____

_____

_____

_____

_____

_____

_____

_____

_____

_____

○ **Pressing through fear**

_____

_____

_____

_____

_____

_____

_____

_____

_____

_____

_____

_____

_____

o Money, Impact and Freedom

_____

_____

_____

_____

_____

_____

_____

_____

_____

_____

_____

_____

_____

6. What's your vision for your business- next two-year plan?

_____

_____

_____

_____

_____

_____

_____

_____

_____

_____

_____

_____

_____

Call to Action and Conclusion

As you explore every facet of your life, Queen, I am very proud of you, and honored if you would entrust me to serve as your coach. I remind my Queens that two things remain true when you are working through life's process:

1. Life is messy and you might feel yanked away from your throne, but if you keep coming back to your vision, your goal, and your God-given purpose in this life, you will succeed.

2. It is easy to charge forward with all of the principles and concepts in this book and let them all slip away and disappear and forget your crown.

I, as a fellow **Queen Boss** rising, command you not to do so. I see **Greatness** in you. It is time that the world sees it too.

Today, I pass to you your scepter, so that you walk graciously through your kingdom to sit on your throne with relentless visions brimming over with tenacity and intention to make major impact with yourself and with others.

Remember, you are a Queen Boss rising, own it!

"Always wear your Invisible Crown."

With Love,

Erica Stepteau

The Queen Boss Rise

Get the Support & Mentorship you Need...

Tenacious Queen Academy team is equipped to serve women who are in the <u>building</u> stages **AND** <u>scaling</u> stages of their business.

TENACIOUS QUEEN TRACK:

You are the Queen who has not achieved consistent $5,000 months in business. You need ample support and guidance in building a sustainable and profitable business. Below you will see all the resources to help you obtain clarity of your ideal client, niche, and building a solid 2-year business plan.

TQ Inner Circle: Tenacious Queen Inner Circle is a membership space for those who value the connection of Queen Sisters as they up level their life and business. This space is perfect to learn and apply the Positioned2Influence Sales System in order to ERADICATE generational poverty curses and become a 6-Figure, Queen Boss! In addition, you will have access to an exclusive membership site which houses video modules, quarterly VIP sessions with a TQA Coach. You will ALSO have access to LIVE Masterminds facilitated by our Master Sales Coach, Erica Stepteau every month to achieve the financial success you desire AND deserve!

Join The Inner Circle Today!

www.TQInnerCircle.com

QUEEN BOSS TRACK:

You are the Queen who has achieved consistent clients totaling close to $5,000 per month or more. You need ample support and guidance in scaling your profit-generating business. Below you will see all the resources to help you become a Queen B.O.S.S (Master of Budgets, Operations, Systems, Sales).

12-Month Queen Boss Behavior Mastermind: Queen Boss Behavior Mastermind is a program to scale your business by using the framework and results you have achieved with your clients. We will develop full cycle funnels from lead generation to sales conversion systems. You will get direct support from our Master Sales Coach who will be your COO of your business; In addition, Tech, Content, and Book Publishing support from the TQA team. This program also includes publicity opportunities to massively increase your brand exposure: Magazine cover/publications, Paid Speaking gigs. Podcast interview bookings, and TV appearances.

About the Authors

Tahira Best is an electric, award-winning, International Speaker and Author who coaches women to overcome internal obstacles and be the best version of themselves. As a Transformational Coach, Tahira attracts women who are ready to embark on the journey of self-love and appreciation. As a speaker, Tahira has had the opportunity to move her audiences at corporate events, conferences, and workshop seminars. Her reputation as a no-nonsense transformational coach has allowed women to boldly love themselves via Best's bold messages and authentically connected accountability. Through her attentive and passionate understanding of her clients, Best is continuously inspired and reminded she is aligned with her purpose.

Best's most notable award to date is the International Award-Winning Speaker- Exceptional Woman of Excellence from the Women's Economic Forum. Tahira's personal ability to overcome obstacles both personal and professional has fueled her to provide innovative solutions and implement the most effective practices to fulfill each client's needs. Her expertise is backed by years of training and experience to empower people to unapologetically define, embrace, and share their greatness with the world. Through this, her clients can love themselves more, refine their self-confidence, and discover their untapped talents and infinite potential.

When Tahira is not speaking at engagements or empowering others, she is traveling, coaching cheerleading, and spending time with her family. Her motto is a quote by Lisa Nichols, "It ain't ever too late to press reset and fall madly in love with the life that you've been given." What is it that keeps Tahira going: knowing the person she can be, keeps her committed to be a lifelong learner with something to chase?

To learn more about Tahira Best and become a part of a community:

https://www.facebook.com/illuminatedqueens

https:www.facebook.com/groups/illuminatedqueens

https://www.tahirabest.com

❧

Morgan Edwards is an award-winning Tech Strategist who helps small business owners streamline their businesses to maximize their profits. Also known as Your Chief Tech Officer, Morgan's focus is 'Creating Impact Together', through said partnerships to provide business owners the freedom to achieve a higher bottom line. Morgan's education and 5 plus years in Information Technology provide her clients with the reassurance they will reduce the frustrations of technology and seamlessly focus on the very thing that brought their business to fruition. One of Morgan's most notable awards to date is the Award of Excellence, presented by the Tenacious Queen Academy. Through her business, she ensures the following: management of systems and processes, landing pages that convert, and balancing the analytical aspects and creativity of technology.

"I don't do just tech- I partner with women and leverage technology to help spread their massive missions." -Edwards

❧

Dr. Jackie Evans Phillips, Doctor of Education with a Masters in Clinical Psychology, making a difference in the lives of others has become Dr. Jackie life's purpose. Passing the torch of greatness has become a personal mission both in her public and private life.

Life Changers' Writers and Healing Institute LLC, is a company that empowers and transforms individuals to be Life Changers These are individuals who are ready to ignite their warrior spirit by understanding the meaning of their life's journey to create impact within their communities and marketplace by documenting and sharing their stories and books.

As a Mid-Wife of Purpose and Best Seller, Dr. Jackie continues to awaken individuals to their Call to Greatness through her books, seminars, trainings and motivational speeches. Dr. Jackie has written four books, The Power of the Valley, Soaring into Greatness, The Greatness within You and The Purpose Factor. In addition, she participated in two book compilations Stand up to be Heard and Women Across Borders. Her books continue to serve as tools for her clients and complements her seminars.

Dr. Jackie is on a personal mission through the I Am ... My Story Campaign to create an empowerment movement of individuals who are ready to be awaken to their Call to Greatness. Through this moment she has empowered many these Life Changers have become authors. The Life Changers Writers and Healing Institue provides writing coaching and publishing services for individuals who are interested in writing their books or writing a chapter in Dr. Jackie's Book Project.

Dr. Jackie has 16 years as an educator and currently works as an adjunct faculty in the MS program in Higher Education at Post University and Central Connecticut State University in the field of higher education.

Visit our website, www.drjackiephillips.com for additional information.

Ayingi Kimble

Born on the small island of Jamaica, Ayingi Kimble's life has been the ultimate example of perseverance and a willingness to help others. Despite a difficult childhood under the shadows of a mother who committed suicide and suffering from *keratoconus* that affected her most of her school years, Ayingi has overcome and has discovered her knack for working with people. She is frequently described as a good listener, to whom family, friends and colleagues turn to for advice.

Ayingi believes there is value in every life and her experience as a "victim" of suicide has given her a passion for helping victims and survivors of suicide and other loss experiences.

She is a firm believer in applying Bible based principles and teaching to solving everyday issues. She was motivated to do coaching after having been employed at Choose Life International, an agency that helps victims of suicide.

Her determination to lead others through trauma has led to transformational experiences.

Kimble's phrase to life is, "Get out of your way and seek to understand before seeking to be Understood." Ayin Life Ministries, created by Kimble, empowers those who have lost a loved one due to suicide or other trauma to not just survive but thrive. Providing her people with tools to give themselves a second chance after experiencing loss, individuals can redesign their happiness to thrive in life.

Kimble has a certificate in Suicide Prevention from Choose Life International. She is a certified life coach. She has also received awards from Choose Life International in appreciation of her professional, compassionate, and dedicated service to helping people live.

In her free time, Kimble enjoys inspirational reading, spending time with her family, writing, or sitting by the ocean listening to the waves while eating a sweetsop.

🪷

Srebrenica Lejla is a Copywriter & Strategist for emerging entrepreneurs, Lifestyle Blogger, and Creative Mentor. Individuals are taught to Discover the Creator Within and can place themselves on authentic platforms for their stories to be acknowledged. Starting with her victories of writing and pitching to publications with large followings, Lejla knew there were others who desired the same. In her supportive Facebook Group, The Lively Creatives, individuals can share their art, successes, and struggles with creating and sharing their work. She has also had success with implementing The Creative's VMA Course, which walks writers through the process of visualizing, monetizing, and actualizing their goals as writers. Through this, people in her community can reap the benefits of powerful collaborations, for she believes there is much power in unity. Her first published book was inspired by her Lifestyle Blog, www.thelivelycreative.com, focusing on mental health, life inspiration, and some of her crafty projects.

Srebrenica Lejla also specifically helps business owners convey their brands to provide magnetic messaging that converts into profits. Many businesses are sitting on gold mines and just magic words to connect with their people. Lejla also includes group and coaching to help writers understand their creative process and create effective time management for their writing. You may even catch her written work in *The Queen Boss Rise Anthology*, sharing her experiences and lessons learned as an emerging entrepreneur. Just from taking the courage to get back in the habit of putting pen to paper, Lejla has excelled by becoming a two-time author in less than a year. As an MBA candidate, Srebrenica Lejla also enjoys crafty DIY projects, baking sweet treats, and exploring around the world.

You can learn more about Srebrenica Lejla and The Lively Creative via:

Email: sb@thelivelycreative.com

www.thelivelycreative.com

FB/IG: @srebrenicalejla

❧

Larkeia Keyonna Matthews is the CEO/ Founder of H.E.R Legacy in HEELS, a national Empowerment coaching and training business.

Larkeia started her professional education in Psychology and Business at Victory University in Memphis, TN. Since childhood, Larkeia has had a natural love for the written word and helping others. After the profound hearing loss of her oldest son, Larkeia was faced with a setback in her formal education. She had to pause her education. She decided to be totally available for her son's recovery, all the while devising a strategy to bounce back and create a new path to her goals.

Before deciding to create H.E.R Legacy in 2017, Larkeia informally educated herself for 4 years in areas of personal growth and development, Spirituality, universal laws, the art of Speaking and coaching. She attended online campuses, enrolled in programs and seminars offered by some of the country's most influential leaders, such as Lisa Nichols, John Maxwell, Eric Thomas, Dr. Maricia Sherman, and sales strategist Erica Stepteau.

There's no wonder why Larkeia Matthews is such a rising star in the empowerment and personal development industry, she has Tenaciously Overcome adversities untold, gleaned from and joined forces with powerful movers and shakers in the industry. She is a growing triple threat, Author, Transformational speaker, and Personal Power/Mindset coach.

Larkeia specializes in the use of divine wisdom coupled with spiritual laws and strategies to retrain the brain, equip you to walk in your divinity and allow you take your power back! Her specialty is designed for women and youth.

Aside from being a powerhouse, she is a wife and a mother of five. Motherhood was her claimed catalyst and breeding ground of her divine assignment. Her heart's desire is for every and anyone to live a life filled with purpose and passion while growing themselves.

Larkeia also attributes the start of her spiritual journey to her family's deep roots in spirituality since her childhood. Her family's church is where her spiritual giftings were discovered and trained. She spearheaded the development of their first youth ministry and served as its director for two years. After her assignment was completed, she continued to mentor young adults in her community.

HER Legacy Hosts youth vision board workshops throughout the year Called Dare to Dream, Dare to Be! Her motto is, "The children are our future, so let's help them create a beautiful one!" This dynamic woman wears her heart on her sleeve as she empowers and equips teens and Queens down the path of Emerging from their ashes to own their divinity and walk in their God-given powers!

You may connect with her via

Facebook: @uplevelme or Larkeia Matthews

email Larkeia.1Legacy@gmail.com

Linked In & Instagram: Larkeia Matthews

❧

Dr. Karen Maxfield-Lunkin, Award-winning #WriteRemedyCoach, Best-selling visionary author, and educational entrepreneur. With more than 25 years as a teacher, school principal, professor, educational advocate, and parent-coach, Dr. Karen has helped transform many lives through her work. She is also the founder of BridgeUcation Creative Consulting Group, advocating for creative collaboration through writing; the Women Writing2Heal International Retreats and the Write2Heal: Creative, Critical Self-Reflection Writing Model to inspire women (and men) to write their stories. Dr. Karen resides in Austin, Texas with her husband Michael of 31 years, and is an adjunct professor at a Texas university.

Dr. Karen hosts workshops, retreats, online courses and YouTube demonstrations for writing. She coaches a clientele of writers which range from the most reluctant of writers to seasoned authors who simply need her push.

Dr. Karen's current initiative is the *Write2Heal: The African Roots Project Ghana Retreat*. During this fantastic journey, participants are led through a healing process that is like no other. Dr. Karen's mission is to *"help women uncover to discover to recover their God-given gifts and talents buried deep within them"*. As a thought leader and innovator, Dr. Karen's aspiration of becoming a writing therapist through this project has come into fruition. She believes the process of writing allows our thoughts and feelings to become visible, so that we may acknowledge them. The cathartic effect of seeing such words form on paper initiates that transformation. Dr. Karen and Mike have three adult children and two insanely cute rescue dogs

Working from the premise of healing through critical self-reflection, Dr. Karen's clients can peel back the layers needed through writing. Dr. Karen is heart centered around women of color over the age of 50 who are ready to step into their entrepreneurial endeavors. When Dr. Karen is not out helping transform lives through writing, she enjoys spending time with family, reading, sing, and making her famous *best cheesecakes in the world.*

You can learn more about the *Write2Heal Women's Retreat & African Roots Project, Ghana trip* via
https://www.facebook.com/events/2240319769348799/
https://www.facebook.com/Dr.KayBridge/?modal=admin_todo_tour
https://www.bridgeucation.com

Contact Info: bridgeucation88@gmail.com

🪷

Cindy May is a fashion stylist who also has a knack for savvy financial keeping. As a blogger, fashion stylist and financial coach, Cindy ensures women look and feel confident about their appearance and their finances. She is all about the glam life! One of the most rewarding aspects of her career is helping women take control of their life by tending to their needs and wants. She coaches courageous women that have the willpower to advance to the next level in life. Cindy is dedicated to helping women build confidence because it is an important key to success. Glam is important to her because it's an expression of individuality and creativity. Cindy is also a co-author of the Queen Boss Rise Anthology which includes unique stories of over 15 women on their entrepreneurial journey. She has also received certificate of recognition for business training at a corporate financial institution. Fashion styling has been a focus of Cindy since her childhood and she later merged her love for fashion with her career in finances to merge the gap between the two. Cindy encourages women to look stunning and have financial security. Cindy has a passion to help people push beyond their fears and rise to greatness. Her mantra is to never give up! You can learn more about Cindy May via
www.bosscqueen.wordpress.com,Facebook/Instagram @bosscqueens or email Bosscqueens@gmail.com

🪷

Brittney Moffat is an award-winning content writer and social media strategist who helps entrepreneurs grow their influence, visibility and engaged audience through consistent lead-generating content! Her mission is to help women find their voice and speak confidently about their mission. She's an ambitious millennial who started blogging to share her experiences and further her career. Her blog, *According to Brittney*, ultimately up-leveled her career, life and helped her start her own freelancing marketing business. According to Brittney guides women through "adulting," entrepreneurship and marketing. She has worked with brands such as Uber, U.S. News and World Report, Dollar Tree and more! She helps women grow their brands daily through her Facebook Group, Content Marketing for Women Entrepreneurs, Bloggers and Influencers. Outside of her business and blog, she resides in Cleveland, Ohio with her boyfriend and cat/fur child, Luna. She enjoys being involved in the community, meeting new people and traveling! Most of all, she loves whenever she gets the chance to play her favorite video game, the Sims! She gives everyone she meets a "pink and sparkly perspective to content marketing!" Popular Saying: "It's time to grow your influence, visibility and engaged audience through content marketing!" Title: Content Writer and Social Media Strategist Mission Statement: To help women entrepreneurs find their voice and speak confidently about their message.

Website: AccordingtoBrittney.com

Social Media:

https://www.facebook.com/accordingtobrittney/
https://www.facebook.com/groups/765889460238111/
https://www.instagram.com/accordingtobrittney/
https://twitter.com/According2Brit
https://www.pinterest.com/according2brit/

Contact info: contact@accordingtobrittney.com

❧

Jacinta Parris is an award-winning Virtual Assistant to busy female entrepreneurs. She specializes in administrative, social media and lifestyle management. Jacinta also coaches other aspiring VA's on how to build a lasting business with a higher purpose. She has enjoyed every exciting moment of growing her business!

Jacinta's journey began right after college when she and a high school friend started up a residential and commercial cleaning business. That summer, they spent many long days and nights dreaming of ways to make the business a success. In the space of no time, they began getting more business than the two could handle. They became overwhelmed with all the paperwork; follow-ups; appointment setting; staff hiring, and the list continued to grow. Life took a different turn for her business partner and soon Jacinta found herself managing the business on her own. There were times when she just wanted to quit and walk away but something kept telling her it will pay off in the end, and it did!

Even with the excitement of the growing business, Jacinta knew she would need help with the number of tasks she also had to manage. It was during this time that Jacinta found her first virtual assistant. Jacinta's assistant took on all the time-consuming tasks and allowed her to concentrate solely on her area of genius. She began to realize using the virtual assistant was also helping her balance her own life and personal well- being. She discovered her true passion was to assist other women in protecting the greatest assets they owned: Themselves!

Love Life Virtual Solutions began as Jacinta's way of helping women gain the sort of work/life balance most women crave. Virtual assistance is more than just helping with tasks; it is about helping women achieve their goals while they enjoy the fruits of their labor.

That was 2 years ago. Since then, Jacinta has worked with many amazing and ambitious women, Fortune 500 companies, as well as aspiring Virtual Assistants. All have amazing visions and dreams for the future of their business. Jacinta loves the feeling she gets when she is able to be a part of someone's dream, saving them valuable time by taking some of the weight off their shoulders.

As a Virtual Assistant coach, Jacinta also teaches other Virtual Assistants the value and purpose of the service they provide to entrepreneurs. Her teachings assist Virtual Assistants in taking their business to the next level while maintaining balance in their own amazing lives.

✿

Aisha Quinn (founder of Queen Boss) dedicates her life to helping black women and young people of color discover their talents and develop their confidence to implement their skills. As a living testimony to overcoming life's challenges, she believes that buried beneath each broken heart is a diamond waiting to show off its beauty to the world. With over 10 years of experience working in correctional environments, Aisha knows first-hand what happens to a person who loses hope in themselves and the people around them.

✿

Erica Stepteau is a Growth and Sales Strategist who empowers Tenacious Queens to create more impact, money, and freedom in their lives. She accomplishes this living by the mottos of #NoQueenLeftBehind & #NoCoinLeftBehind. Owner of the Tenacious Queen Academy, LLC, Stepteau creates powerful experiences for women business owners to maximize their profits while excelling in their realm of expertise. Stepeau's current recognitions include the 2019 Boss Lady of Year & Female Advocate/Activist of the Year Nominee.

In her Facebook Group, Tenacious Queens Unite, there is a multitude of women who are typically in 3 different stages of their business: New, Established, and Shifting. Stepteau offers women business owners the opportunity to meet in person and gain one of a kind insights to take themselves to the next level. The Tenacious Queen Profit Incubators are held throughout the year across the nation and has proven to help women take immediate action and excel in their businesses.

Stepteau's career history includes highlights of Communications Expert in Human Resources and Sales Trainer at Wells Fargo. She has utilized her experience to create a unique sisterhood connection with her people, "I have a great gift and skill set in connecting people and identifying talent for my clients. When my clients book with me or invest in Tenacious Queen Academy programs they immediately obtain partnerships, exposure opportunities, new clients, and biz besties!" When Stepteau isn't in her Queen of Sales mode you can catch her playing Rock Band, delving into Interior Design, and Netflix binging.

Stepteau has built a dynamic Tenacious Queen tribe that is like no other. Her success has been proven to help Queens earn consistent income and master the art of selling. The unity and support in her tribe is unmatched, resulting in client retention rates over 80%. In 2018 alone her clients collectively earned over 1 million dollars in revenue.

You can learn more about the Tenacious Queen Academy at www.TenaciousQueenAcademy.com

❁

Sabrina Thomas is an author, speaker, advocate and also an IEP coach with a passion for working with families with special needs children. She knows firsthand how overwhelming life can be, which is why she finds joy in speaking about what she has learned and sharing her life with others

She has co-authored two books: *Moments in Life, The Caregiver's Story*, and *You Need It; I Got It!* both of which share her life experiences, challenges, and growth strategies as a special need parent. She is currently co-authoring several other books that will be published later this year.

One of the most rewarding parts of her career stems from being able to give parents, families and caregivers the power and knowledge they need to be their child's best advocate.

Sabrina Thomas is filled with enough enthusiasm and compassion to be the voice of the voiceless. She believes that every parent has the capacity to be an advocate for their children, which is why she spends her time joyfully sharing her experiences and lessons with others.

Spending time with family, volunteering for various organizations and building her business are among her greatest pleasures. As an entrepreneur she finds immense joy in continuing her education and helping others along the way and enriching life would certainly be an added bonus. Her mission is to ensure special needs families never go at it alone and always feel supported.

She is the proud mother of two sons, one of whom is a special needs child and the major inspiration which drives her passion. Spending most of her spare time with her son has given her enough understanding of what it takes to care for those children with special needs, and she is glad to share this understanding with anyone in need.

⚜

Lindsey Vertner, Award-winning Personal Development Coach experienced a "fatal" car wreck in 2007 which had multiple medics pronouncing Lindsey brain dead and paralyzed. Amongst a multitude of injuries and battling to live, Lindsey acquired a rare outlook on life. As a personal development coach, she uses her unparalleled perspective to push her clients towards success. Lindsey has a gift for teaching people how to unlock their potential and step into their greatness! Founder of Lindsey Vertner, LLC, she is devoted to teaching leaders how to create a life full of purpose, balance, and happiness by empowering them to practice self-care while creating boundaries, to prioritize their goals while avoiding burnout and overwhelm, and to gain personal growth while healing limiting beliefs. She teaches the overwhelmed woman how to balance her life by putting herself first without guilt. As a nonprofit co-founder of The Unleashed Woman, Lindsey helps to support and uplift women through empowerment and networking events. Looking to help clients in all areas of their lives, Lindsey partnered with Max Credit Score to become a credit building strategist – helping clients to reach credit scores of 700 or higher while providing educational tools to help maintain positive financial habits for the long term.

As a captivating speaker and leadership consultant, not only does she motivate and inspire her audience, but she challenges and encourages them to lean on her and act immediately. Lindsey serves by speaking life into others by utilizing her inspirational experiences to provide practical and actionable tips. She facilitates private workshops in the areas of leadership development, stress management, and time management/productivity. Authoring her forthcoming book, "When Great Isn't Good Enough", Lindsey aims to help readers turn their losses into lessons. With a master's in Professional Counseling & Coaching, Lindsey is a graduate of both Indiana University and Liberty University.

Learn more about Lindsey and her services and products at www.LindseyVertner.com and www.TheUnleashedWoman.net. Connect with her on social media at @LindseyVertner on Facebook, Instagram, and Twitter. Subscribe to her YouTube channel at www.youtube.com/LindseyVertnerLLC

Tiffany Williams: Health Coach! Tiffany Williams-Parra is a Fitness Trainer, Healthy Eats Foodie, and Owner of Phoenix Fitness Fanatics. Renewing herself after a major 100lb weight shedding, Tiffany's motivation and passion is to help others become reborn through health transformations ignited. When it comes to her fitness journey, Tiffany's mother and son have been the highest inspiration. The value of working hard and pushing through adversity to achieve desired results reaps the best benefits. Tiffany has learned to rise above adversities, regardless of the situation and knows it is possible to conquer anything!

Throughout Tiffany's experience with her clients, she notices the biggest struggle is the momentum to get moving. She correlates this struggle due from simply the fear of not knowing what to do to become and stay fit. She teaches her clients to show up, no matter what! She leads by example by staying social, sharing her journey of the things she does personally to stay fit. Her passion for fully connecting with her clients allows her to seamlessly help create routines she knows they will stick to.

Phoenix Fitness Fanatics key unique point is helping clients make healthier food choices while navigating through a busy life. Tiffany provides lucrative ideas to switch bad foods for healthier options so her clients can eat with confidence. Her commitment to healthy living doesn't stop at the physical aspect. To help her clients learn all the steps needed to for a Healthy Lifestyle Transformation, she will be hosting her first Annual Women's Recharge, Release, and Reset Retreat, May 17th - 19th, 2019, in the tranquil mountains of Big Bear California with future destinations already in the works.

In her free time, Tiffany loves going to the gym to further her own health transformation. She calls it her "Therapy". She also enjoys hiking with friends, visiting local wineries, and attending Reggae concerts with her husband. Parra admits, she finds the most joy in running 5K runs with her son. Sometimes she even lets him win. If there is nothing else, Tiffany gets inspired by the expression "When you feel like quitting, remember why you started!"

To learn more about Tiffany and Phoenix Fitness Fanatics visit her on one of her social media sites.

Website: www.phoenixfitfans.com
Instagram: Phoenixfitnessfanaticscoachit
Facebook Business Page: www.facebook.com/PFFCoachIT/
Facebook Group Page:
https://www.facebook.com/groups/373719946381942/

67757826R00087

Made in the USA
Columbia, SC
31 July 2019